Tudor and Stuart Texts

The Queen's Majesty's Passage

Tudor and Stuart Texts

Series Editor

Katherine Acheson
Department of English, University of Waterloo

This is a series of modernized scholarly editions of important English Renaissance and Reformation texts, published by the Centre for Reformation and Renaissance Studies. The series emphasizes texts which have not been produced in modern editions and whose availability will contribute to ongoing attempts to interpret and to teach the English Renaissance.

Titles published

The True Law of Free Monarchies and *Basilikon Doron*
James I. Ed. Daniel Fischlin and Mark Fortier

The Trial of Nicholas Throckmorton
Ed. Annabel Patterson

Early Stuart Pastoral: The Shepherd's Pipe *by William Browne and others and* The Shepherd's Hunting *by George Wither*
Ed. James Doelman

The Queen's Majesty's Passage & Related Documents
Ed. Germaine Warkentin

For a list of CRRS publications, see page 159

Cover: Detail from the 'Coronation portrait' of Elizabeth I. This painting of ca. 1600 is based on an earlier one of about 1559, in which Elizabeth was painted in the gown she wore on the day of her entry. She is shown wearing the imperial crown (see Introduction). By courtesy of the National Portrait Gallery, London.

Title page ornament: A popular emblematic printer's device: 'Time rescuing Truth from Calumny.' *From The Historie of Philip de Commines, knight, Lord of Argenton.* (London: Imprinted by Ar. Hatfield, for I. Norton, 1601), 224. STC 5603. Centre for Reformation and Renaissance Studies, Victoria University in the University of Toronto.

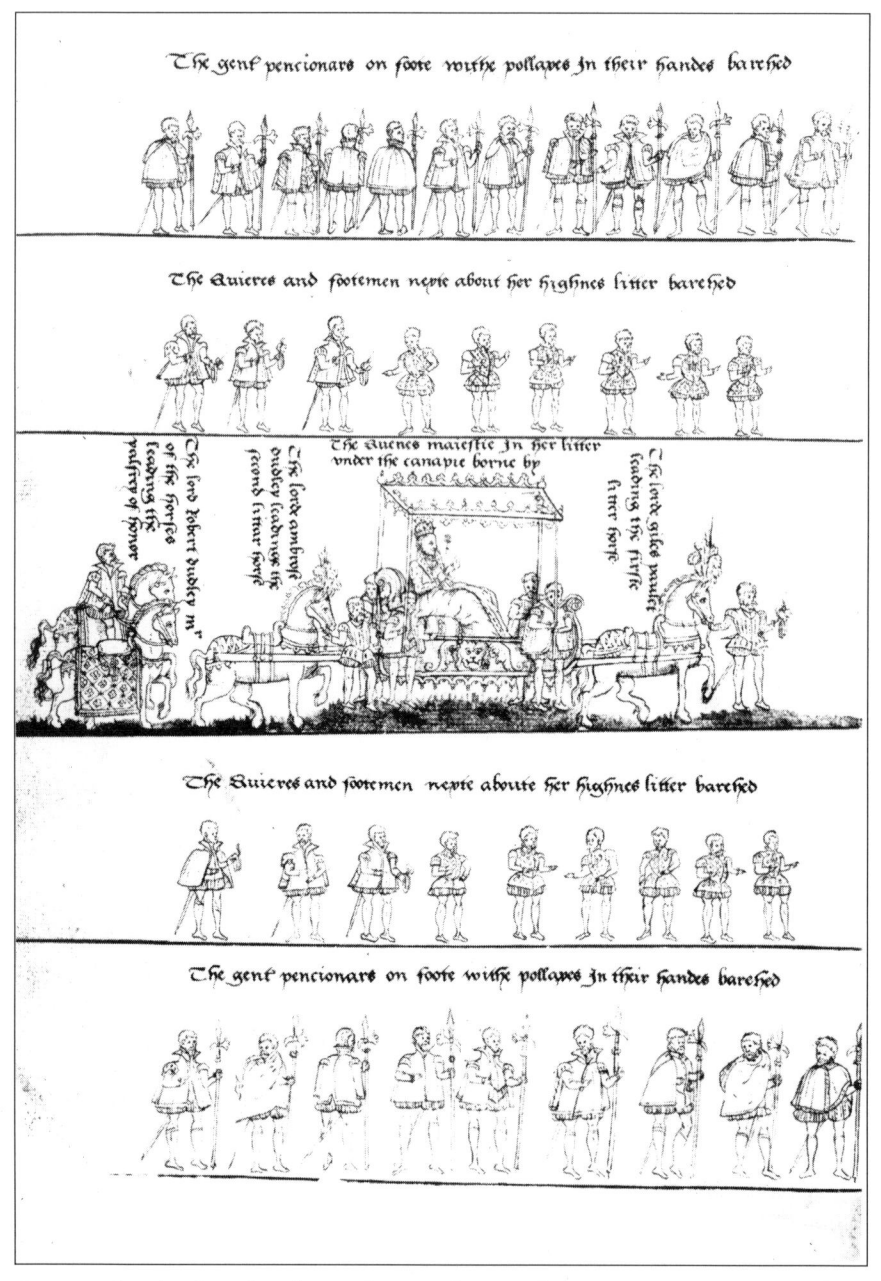

Queen Elizabeth in her litter during during the procession into London, January 14, 1558. College of Arms ms. M.6, f.41^v. By permission.

The Queen's Majesty's Passage
& Related Documents

Edited, Modernized, and with an Introduction by
GERMAINE WARKENTIN

Assisted by
JOHN CARMI PARSONS

Toronto
Centre for Reformation and Renaissance Studies
2004

CRRS Publications
Centre for Reformation and Renaissance Studies
Victoria University in the University of Toronto
Toronto, Canada M5S 1K7

© 2004 by the Centre for Reformation and Renaissance Studies
All rights reserved.

National Library of Canada Cataloguing in Publication

The Queen's Majesty's passage & related documents / Germaine Warkentin, editor.

(Tudor and Stuart texts)
Includes bibliographical references and index.
ISBN 0-7727-2024-X

    1. Elizabeth, Queen of England, 1533-1603—Coronation.
2. Processions—England—London—History—16th century—Sources.
3. Coronations—Great Britain—History—16th century—Sources.
I. Warkentin, Germaine, 1933– II. Victoria University (Toronto, Ont.). Centre for Reformation and Renaissance Studies. III. Series.

DA350.Q43 2004   941.05'5'092   C2004-902364-0

No part of this book may be translated or reproduced in any form, by print, photoprint, microfilm, or any other means, without written permission from the publisher.

Cover design: Paragraphics, Toronto

Typesetting and print production by Becker Associates, Toronto.

Contents

List of Illustrations	9
Acknowledgements	11
Introduction	15
The Receiving of the Queen's Majesty	75
Appendix I: Contemporary Narratives of Elizabeth's Entry	99
Appendix II: Documents Relating to the Queen's Entry, 1558-1559	115
Appendix III: Translations of Latin Passages	127
Glossary and Gazetteer	133
Textual Note	139
Bibliography	143
Index	153

Illustrations

Detail from the 'Coronation portrait' of Elizabeth I — Cover
Frontispiece: The Queen in her litter during the royal entry procession — 4
'Time Rescuing Truth from Calumny' — title page

Figures:

1: Title page of *The Quenes maiesties passage through the citie of London to Westminster the daye before her coronacion* (London: Richard Tottel, 1559) — 17
2: First page of the printed text of *The Quenes maiesties passage* — 18
3: 'Allegory of the Tudor Succession: the Family of Henry VIII' — 30
4: Payment to Walter Fyshe for altering the Queen's dress — 34
5a: Gog and Magog surrounded by the Company of Young Freemen, the Lord Mayor's Show, 2002 — 36
5b: The Children of Christ's Hospital marching in the Lord Mayor's Show, 2002 — 36
6: 7 December 1558: The Aldermen allocate pageant responsibilities — 38
7: March 4, 1559: Payment for 'making the book' to Richard Mulcaster — 42

8:	3 January 1559: the Queen's warrant to Sir Thomas Cawarden, Master of the Revels, for the loan of costumes	46
9:	The routes of the November 28 and January 14 processions through the City	47
10:	Braun and Hogenberg, 1572 map of London (detail)	50
11:	Edward VI passes the Cheapside Cross during his entry in 1547	51
12:	Title page of 'The Byble in Englysshe' (London, 1539)	60
13:	St. Michael le Querne, with the Little Conduit (Ralph Treswell, 1585)	62
14:	The figures of Time and Truth from the title page of William Whittingham, *The Newe Testament of Our Lord Iesus Christ* (Geneva, 1557)	64

Acknowledgements

My interest in Elizabeth I's 1559 royal entry into London began some years ago when I was searching for a text that would illustrate to students why the processions and allegories in Edmund Spenser's *The Faerie Queene* would have been moderately intelligible, and certainly interesting, to its contemporary readers, who were regular participants in and witnesses of solemn public processions. *The Queen's Majesty's Passage* proved to be ideal; not only did it present a procession 'richly furnish'd' with allegorical material, but its text was reportedly composed by Spenser's old schoolmaster at Merchant Taylor's School in London. As time went on I explored London with a map of the procession in hand, broadened my interest from the allegories in the pageants to the ritual structure of the entry itself, to its complex historical background (including that of earlier entries), to its history as a printed book, and to the later historiography of the entry. The modernized text of the pamphlet and related documents in this edition provides an opportunity to bring these materials together for the modern reader, as well as a few opportunities to connect the geography and customs of mid-Tudor London with the City as it exists today. Perhaps others will take time to follow the processional route with map in hand, track a historic City company on its web site, or attend November's Lord Mayor's Show, which still contains a few elements featured in the royal entries of English sovereigns.

In work that has taken well over a decade, I have incurred many obligations it is a pleasure to acknowledge here. Most of all I am indebted to the Yale Elizabethan Club, who early permitted their unique copy of the first known edition of the royal entry pamphlet to serve as copy text. I am grateful to John Carmi Parsons, an early collaborator in the project, particularly for his draft translation of the Latin passages in the entry, and to Victoria University for a long-ago grant in aid of that work. Other important contributors to the project have been Dale Hoak of William and Mary College, who drew my attention to some historical work which was new to me, Konrad Eisenbichler who oversaw my revised translation of Aloisio Schivenoglia's letter about the procession, Anne Lancashire who generously shared with me her work on the records of the Corporation of London, Randall McLeod who gave shrewd advice about the copy-text, Abigail Young of the Records of Early English Drama who corrected many mis-transcriptions in the documents, and Edward H. Dahl and John Warkentin who advised on the maps. I am also indebted to Carolyn King of the York University Cartography Laboratory for preparing the route map of the procession, and Ingrid Smith who typed some materials at an early stage.

All or parts of the manuscript were read by Dale Hoak, Alexandra F. Johnston, and – to my delight – my former students Katherine Acheson, Joseph L. Black and Lisa Celovsky, who were cheerfully ruthless in improving the work of their old professor. Parts of the Introduction were first argued in a paper presented at the Renaissance Society of America's conference in 2003. Two anonymous readers for the Aid to Scholarly Publications Programme of the Canadian Federation for the Humanities and Social Sciences gave valuable advice at a late stage, for which my thanks. To all I am very grateful; I have tried to accept as many of their suggestions as possible, but take full responsibility for the final result.

In addition I have incurred specific debts to the following, to all of whom I am very grateful: An Sonjae (Brother Anthony, of Taizé), Jayne Archer, W.W. Barker, Peter Blayney, Clare Browne of the Victoria and Albert Museum, Ursula S. Carlyle, Archivist of the Mercers' Company, Mark Crane, Frédéric Fauquier, Dottoressa Daniela Ferrari of the Archivio di Stato di Mantova, Thomas Izbicki, Carol V. Kaske, Ágnes Juhász-Ormsby, Mark Jurdjevic, John N. King, Sergius Kodera, Gabrielle Langdon, Robert J. Mueller, John H. Munro, Paul V. Murphy, Linda Pellecchia, Jane E. Phillips, Michael Pickard of Hatfield House, Anne-Marie Pyett of the Corporation of the City of London, Scott Schofield, Michael Snow of the Society of Young Freemen, David Townsend, Joseph P. Ward, and Robert Yorke, Archivist of the College of Arms.

In addition to the Yale Elizabethan Club and the Beinecke Library of Yale University, I am grateful for permission to reproduce or cite materials to the following institutions: the National Archives, London (formerly the Public Record Office), the British Library, the British Museum, the College of Arms, the Corporation of the City of London, the National Portrait Gallery, the Society of Antiquaries, the Archivio di Stato di Mantua, the Folger Shakespeare Library, the Huntington Library, the Paul Mellon Collection of the Yale Center for British Art, the Centre for Reformation and Renaissance Studies at Victoria University in the University of Toronto, and the Stewart Museum, Montreal.

This book has been published with the help of a grant from the Canadian Federation for the Humanities and Social Sciences, through the Aid to Scholarly Publications Programme, using funds provided by the Social Sciences and Humanities Research Council of Canada.

Introduction

On January 14 1559, Elizabeth Tudor, Queen of England since the death of her sister Mary on November 17 1558, entered the City of London in ceremonial procession, the traditional prelude to a monarch's coronation at Westminster Abbey on the next day. Following ancient custom she left the Tower of London, processed through the City's streets witnessing pageants at one customary location after another, was ceremonially given a purse of gold coins, and passed beyond the City's western limits at Temple Bar. The crowds who filled the streets for 'the receiving of the Queen's Majesty' saw, many for the first time, an unmarried twenty-five year old red-head, sharply intelligent, highly educated, and as William Camden would later observe, already 'taught by Experience and Adversity.'[1] On the day of the young Queen's entry no one among the religious, court and City factions surrounding her could foretell whether she would survive to rule, or that by the time of her death in 1603, still unmarried, she would become a near-transcendent icon of English majesty. Yet Elizabeth's achievement – in terms of which we habitually read her later mastery back into her early years – had yet to take place. Her contemporaries, as Stephen Alford points out, did not assume the success of the regime was inevitable,[2] and her earliest months as Queen have to be read in the light of that uncertainty, which was at once dynastic, political, religious, and (given the brief reigns of her two predecessors) medical.

Among the men around her Elizabeth had already begun to assert her character in long meetings of the council she had chosen, without doubt in consultation with her secretary William Cecil, later Lord Burghley.[3] The January procession through London aimed to show the Queen to her people, employing a custom they knew well, that of the 'royal entry.' *The Quenes maiesties passage through the citie of London to Westminster the daye before her coronacion. Anno 1558*,[4] published little more than a

---

[1] Camden, *The History of the Most Renowned and Victorious Princess Elizabeth*, 10.
[2] Alford, *The Early Elizabethan Polity*, 28. See also Frye, *Elizabeth I*, vii–viii.
[3] For Elizabeth's appointment of her first council, see MacCaffrey, *Elizabeth I*, 38–42, and Haigh, *Elizabeth I*, 11.
[4] At the time, the English year was sometimes calculated from March 1, so dates in January and February 1559 were dated 1558.

16   The Queen's Majesty's Passage

week later on January 23 (see figures 1 and 2), is a detailed description of that entry, largely composed, it is generally agreed, by the humanist scholar Richard Mulcaster (c. 1532–1611).[5] Himself the son of a Carlisle alderman and born in northern England, Mulcaster was almost exactly the young Queen's contemporary. He was shortly to become both a member of Elizabeth's first parliament, and – as headmaster of Merchant Taylors' School and later St. Paul's – the teacher of the dramatist Thomas Kyd, the poets Thomas Lodge and Edmund Spenser, and the great preacher Lancelot Andrewes. Mulcaster would survive long enough to compose a poem that lamented the Queen's death at the same time as, with the dexterity necessary at court, it celebrated the accession of her successor, James I. Two other figures played important roles in devising and publishing the entry: its probable scenarist, Richard Grafton, the influential London guildsman and chronicler, and Richard Tottel, a stationer with premises in Temple Bar who issued the pamphlet. Tottel specialized in legal books, and he illustrates the typically close links between the personal and the civic that have to be taken into account in understanding life in sixteenth-century London: he was Richard Grafton's son-in-law.[6]

Though the original scenario for the procession – the 'plat' mentioned in the records of the Court of Aldermen (120) – is lost, the occasion and Elizabeth's comportment during it have been preserved for us in not only in the pamphlet but in several narratives, reproduced here in Appendix I: the *Diary* of the London citizen Henry Machyn; the *Chronicle* of Charles Wriothesley, Windsor Herald; the report made to the castellan of Mantua by an Italian living in England, Aloisio Schivenoglia; and a slightly later description existing in two versions, 1562 and 1570, by Richard Grafton himself. From these reports and from the records of London's Court of Aldermen, and to a lesser degree the royal court, (see Appendix II) we can construct a picture of the ritual of the royal entry as it unfolded. Schivenoglia's narrative was written to a fellow-Catholic Italian court official, from an England in which Protestantism was being restored, but it is chiefly concerned with the kind of detail in which a deviser of court ceremonies would be interested. The printed pamphlet was prepared in

---

[5]The text was first attributed to Mulcaster in 1935 by C.R. Baskervill on the basis of the aldermen's payment to him for 'making of the book'('Richard Mulcaster,' 513); for the document see Appendix II and figure 7. See also the more detailed discussion by Strong, 'The 1559 Entry Pageants of Elizabeth I,' in his *The Tudor and Stuart Monarchy: Pageantry, Painting Iconography*, 39–40. This essay reprints chapter I of his frequently cited PhD dissertation, 'Elizabethan Pageantry as Propaganda,' (1962). Despite later research on particular details, Strong's thesis remains the most complete guide to the primary documentation of the entry.

[6]For Tottel's life and connections, see Byrom, 'Richard Tottel – his Life and Work.'

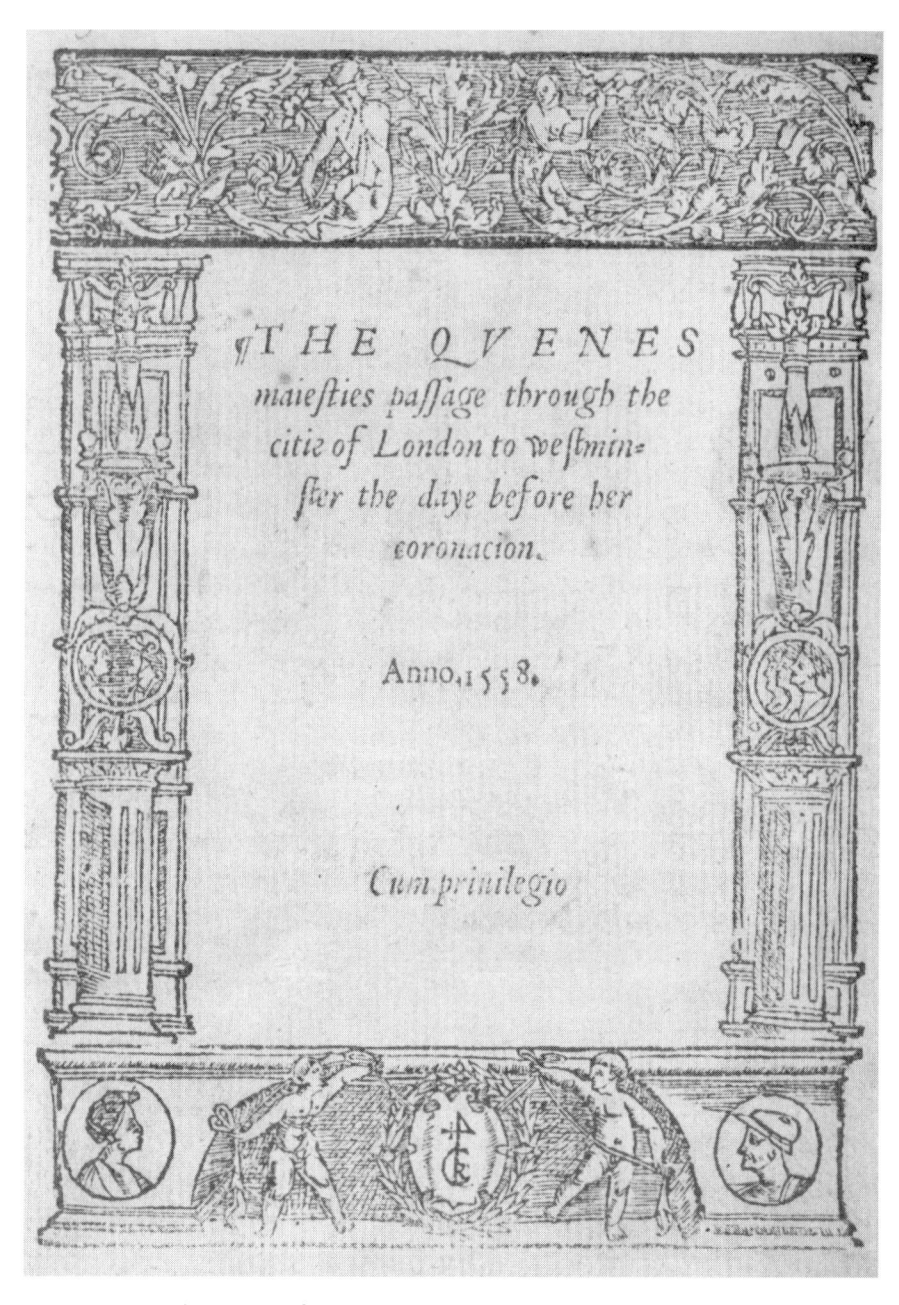

Figure 1: Title page of *The Quenes maiesties passage through the citie of London to Westminster the daye before her coronacion* (London: Richard Tottel, 1559). Yale Elizabethan Club. Yale University: Beinecke Rare Book and Manuscript Library; Eliz. 157.

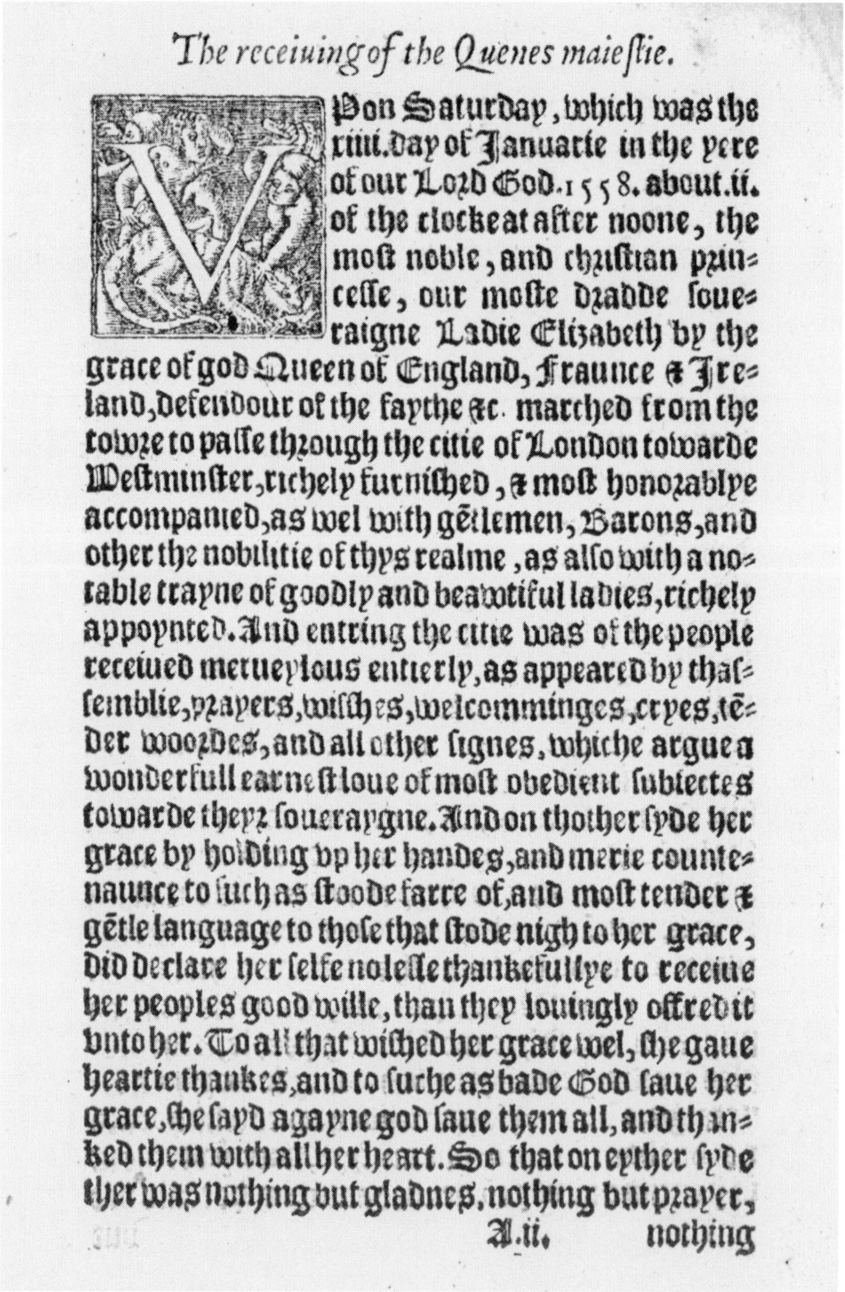

The receiuing of the Quenes maieſtie.

Vpon Saturday, which was the xiiii. day of Januarie in the yere of our Lord God. 1558. about.ii. of the clocke at after noone, the most noble, and christian princesse, our moste dradde soueraigne Ladie Elizabeth by the grace of god Queen of England, Fraunce & Ireland, defendour of the faythe &c. marched from the towre to passe through the citie of London towarde Westminster, richely furnished, & most honorablye accompanied, as wel with gentlemen, Barons, and other the nobilitie of thys realme, as also with a notable trayne of goodly and beawtiful ladies, richely appoynted. And entring the citie was of the people receiued merueylous entierly, as appeared by thassemblie, prayers, wisshes, welcomminges, cryes, tender woordes, and all other signes, whiche argue a wonderfull earnest loue of most obedient subiectes towarde theyr soueraygne. And on thother syde her grace by holding vp her handes, and merie countenaunce to such as stoode farre of, and most tender & gentle language to those that stode nigh to her grace, did declare her selfe nolesse thankefullye to receiue her peoples good wille, than they louingly offred it vnto her. To all that wished her grace wel, she gaue heartie thankes, and to suche as bade God saue her grace, she sayd agayne god saue them all, and thanked them with all her heart. So that on eyther syde ther was nothing but gladnes, nothing but prayer,

A.ii.   nothing

Figure 2: First page of the text of *The Quenes maiesties passage*, f. Aiir. Yale Elizabethan Club. Yale University: Beinecke Rare Book and Manuscript Library; Eliz. 157.

a London circle of enthusiastic evangelicals, but it also constitutes an English parallel to the much grander 'festival books' that recorded continental royal entries. For example, it is deliberately bilingual; the texts of Latin poems spoken or pinned up on the pageants are in the language routinely used by all learned persons in Renaissance Europe. Such publications were of course propaganda, not reportage, and cannot be relied on for factual accuracy. However, comparisons among the various accounts of the 1559 entry suggests that the pamphlet, despite its enthusiastic rhetoric and evident religious and political programme, is fairly accurate as to details. Furthermore, it is possible to learn much about the religious and social culture it represents not only from what the pamphlet explicitly says, but from the implicit information in the design of the procession itself, which drew eclectically on historical precedent, popular motifs, biblical typology, and humanist learning.

'The whole arrangement of a royal entry,' writes R. Malcolm Smuts, '...expressed the coming together of two distinct hierarchies, one based on the wealth created by London's crafts, the other anchored in the traditions of the royal court and the kingdom's great feudal families.'[7] As Roy Strong puts it, 'In one mighty sweep the onlookers saw pass before them, in microcosm, the whole of society as they knew it: the king beneath a canopy attended by his principal officers of state, the nobility, gentry, and knights at arms, the clergy in the form of bishops, priests and the religious orders, the third estate made up of officials and representatives of the guilds and confraternities.'[8] However, though such ritual occasions presented an official drama of social cohesion, all the participants – the Queen, her councillors and noble attendants, the aldermen who greeted her, the citizens who cheered, and not least Grafton and Mulcaster – had agendas of their own to pursue. Though we know more about what happened on January 14, 1559 than many other days of Elizabeth's forty-four year reign, we are still trying to disentangle from the various accounts of the entry what it really signified for those involved, and what it would signify for later historians of the Elizabethan period.

The Ritual of the Monarch's Entry

In the early modern period ceremonies of all sorts enmeshed people 'in a vast support system of socially prescribed activities that helped them through difficult transitions, especially those involving life and death.'[9] One of the most important was that of the transition from one monarch

---

[7] R. Malcolm Smuts, 'Public Ceremony and Royal Charisma,' 73.
[8] Strong, *Art and Power*, 7.
[9] Muir, *Ritual in Early Modern Europe*, 15.

to another; all over Europe and the Middle East cities and towns ceremonially welcomed their ruler at his coronation or when he arrived for a visit. For townspeople living behind high walls there was an important difference between the profane space of the undifferentiated countryside and the sacred space of their city. The city walls and gates were powerful symbols of order in a world of disorder and of justice in the midst of lawlessness.[10] In his *adventus* (arrival, entry), the ruler passed in splendid procession through the great gate to be welcomed by the citizens dressed in their best. Ratified by both classical and biblical example – the Roman triumph, Jesus's entry into Jerusalem on Palm Sunday (John 12, 12–13) – the *adventus* was developed by courts and city-states all over Europe throughout the medieval and Renaissance periods to effect the transition between one reign and the next, or to acknowledge or mediate the power relations between ruler and ruled.[11]

The *adventus*/triumph, however, was far more than a mere display of power; it was an opportunity for the people to counsel their ruler. Medieval chroniclers might present their king as if he were a successful Roman general followed by his captives, riding in his chariot and 'wearing the mantle of Jupiter and crowned with laurel,' but with him there sometimes rode a 'ribald,' a figure ritually sanctioned to mock the *triumphator* and remind him of his limitations.[12] Strong points out that entries 'presented to the ruler himself images of those virtues to which

---

[10] On city gates and their symbolization in the enduring image of the triumphal arch, see Smith, *Architectural Symbolism of Imperial Rome and the Middle Ages*, 11–12, and Rykwert, *The Idea of a Town: the Anthropology of Urban Form in Rome, Italy and the Ancient World*. The capacity of processions to make political and territorial points is evident in today's 'marching season' (around July 12) in conflict-ridden Northern Ireland.

[11] The imagery of the *adventus* has been traced back to descriptions of divine arrival as early as the Homeric 'Hymn to Apollo'; see S. MacCormack, *Art and Ceremony in Late Antiquity*, 18. On the *Adventus* and its close relative the triumph, see Kantorowicz, 'The "King's Advent" and the Enigmatic Panels in the Doors of Santa Sabina.' Gordon Kipling, *Enter the King: Theatre, Liturgy and Ritual in the Medieval Civic Triumph* develops Kantorowicz's argument beyond the Palm Sunday example, arguing that in general medieval entries are informed by the liturgical imagery of Advent. See also M. McCormick, *Eternal Victory: Triumphal Rulership in Late Antiquity, Byzantium and the Early Medieval West*, and more recently – though it has been criticised for errors of fact – Sergio Bertelli, *The King's Body: Sacred Rituals of Power in Medieval and Early Modern Europe*.

[12] Kipling, 'Triumphal Drama: Form in English Civic Pageantry,' 49–50; see also his account of the entry Protestant Edinburgh accorded the Catholic Mary Queen of Scots in 1561, *Enter the King*, 352–356. The ritual humiliation of the entrant probably reached its extreme in the ceremony of the papal *possesso*; see Ingersoll, 'The Possesso, the Via Papale, and the Stigma of Pope Joan.'

he should aspire, and for this the whole tradition of the *speculum principis* or 'mirror of Princes' from St. Augustine to John of Salisbury and the *De Regimine Principum* was drawn upon.'[13] Even the feeblest royal entry was thus a way of giving counsel, its parts intended to work together to achieve a political, and in some cases a moral vision, not of the monarch's rule as it was, but as the presenters would like it to be.[14] In a formal entry the ruler, the elites and the people thus each had a role to play; all were actors in a theatrical spectacle with an important public function.

Renaissance polities – whether in the entries of French kings, the Doge's processions at Venice, the triumphs of the Medici or the elaborate ceremony of the Papal *possesso*[15] – were to an extraordinary degree what the anthropologist Clifford Geertz calls 'theatre states.'[16] *The Queen's Majesty's Passage* openly acknowledges this drama of rule, terming 'the city of London at that time...a stage wherein was shown the wonderful spectacle of a noble-hearted princess toward her most loving people' (78). In continental entries, writes Hans Mielke, 'the sovereign was compared to the gods and heroes of antiquity and so raised to the level of such paragons. Images of illustrious ancestors evoked his noble lineage and gave the stamp of historical event to the ordinary and the commonplace. The new ruler's reign would safeguard agriculture, cause trade to flourish anew, protect from enemies, and...bring forth a new Golden Age, presided over by this virtuous king.'[17] The audience for such a complex

---

[13] Strong, *Art and Power*, 8.

[14] Wilson, *Entertainments for Elizabeth*, 8.

[15] Withington, *English Pageantry*, attempts to list every occasion that purports to be an entry in England before the eighteenth century. For detailed discussion of late-medieval entries in Northern Europe see Kipling, *Enter the King*, passim; many entries are discussed in Bertelli, *The King's Body*, 62–96. For Scotland see Gray, 'The Royal Entry in Sixteenth-Century Scotland.' For Italy see Mitchell, *Italian Civic Pageantry in the High Renaissance* (with a good introduction to the field and many detailed descriptions of entries); for the Papal *possesso*, with wide-ranging bibliography, see also Fosi, 'Court and City in the Ceremony of the *Possesso* in the Sixteenth Century.' For provincial France in a slightly later period see Wagner and Vaillancourt, *Le roi dans la ville*. For Renaissance festivals in general see Strong, *Art and Power: Renaissance Festivals 1450–1650*, with a useful calendar of 'Major Festival Events and Publications, 1494–1641,' 175–179. The essays collected in Jacquot, *Les fêtes de la Renaissance* (1956, 1960) remain important. For the slow decay of the ritual in England after Elizabeth, see below.

[16] See Geertz's influential *Negara: the Theatre State in Nineteenth-Century Bali*. For a comparison of Elizabeth's 1559 entry with parallel examples from Java and Morocco, see his 'Centers, Kings and Charisma: Reflections on the Symbolics of Power.'

[17] Hans Mielke, introduction to Bochius, *The Ceremonial Entry of Ernst, Archduke of Austria, into Antwerp, June 14, 1594*, x.

spectacle was equally complex in its social structure and political concerns: the citizenry delighting in the colour and display but held back by barriers in the streets, the aldermen waiting with their purse of gold at the Little Conduit, the watchful courtiers riding by in their ranks. In a sense even the Queen herself was a spectator at her own welcome, as we shall see. One thing is clear: a royal entry was a great public performance, a spectacle that for a brief time drew all eyes and all energies. In England at least, the noise was deafening; the peoples' shouts and cheers were their way of participating in an occasion which, as their rulers well knew, they could quickly disrupt if they wanted to.[18]

The intellectual elites were equally involved; in helping to devise such events the humanist secretaries of princes and dukes often drew not only on the classical examples that were familiar to them, but on literary models like the widely read *Trionfi* of the fourteenth-century Italian poet Francesco Petrarca. There Petrarch depicts Love, Chastity, Death, Fame, Time, and Eternity, each triumphing one after another over its predecessor.[19] So accepted was the custom of the entry, with its attendant moral-political dimension, that it could be satirized to wicked effect, as the famous Dutch humanist Erasmus showed in his popular dialogue *Julius exclusus* (*Julius Excluded from Heaven*, ca. 1517/18). In it the notoriously worldly pope Julius II, at his death thumps on St. Peter's gates. The saint peers out, complaining that the place smells like a sewer, and asks 'Who are you? What do you want?' to which Julius responds 'I want you to open the doors, and quickly; if you did your job properly, you'd have come out to meet me – with a solemn procession of angels, too.'[20] Europe roared with laughter; *Julius exclusus* went through 13 Latin editions in four months and was rapidly translated into German, English and French.

Over many centuries the details of the ruler's entry would vary according to time and place, but certain elements recur persistently. A procession takes place along a 'sacred' or publicly significant route, the central figure rides or is carried in a litter (often under a canopy), there is a strong visual element – paintings, signs, ceremonial architecture and, by the fifteenth century, pageants[21] – the attendants of the ruler are

---

[18] R. Malcolm Smuts, 'Public Ceremonial and Royal Charisma,' 74–76. And they could, of course, temper their enthusiasm: the crowd was noticeably quiet during Anne Boleyn's entry; see Ives, *Anne Boleyn*, 222.

[19] Petrarch's *Trionfi* were translated into English some time before 1547 by Henry Parker, Lord Morley, and were published in 1554, well before Petrarch's sonnets began to influence Elizabethan poetry; see Bartlett, 'The Occasion of Lord Morley's Translation of the *Trionfi*.'

[20] Erasmus, *Julius Excluded from Heaven*, 168. The dialogue is reliably attributed to Erasmus, though he always avoided acknowledging authorship; see 156–158.

[21] For 'pageant' see Glossary. For the early origins of such visual material see

present in their ranks, and gifts of money are distributed by the ruler, or conversely a purse is presented to the ruler by the town's representatives.[22] These elements are present in *The Queen's Majesty's Passage*, and in a way that suggests that though English scenarists took some time to adopt the classical motifs favoured on the continent,[23] they nevertheless possessed the practical experience, historical awareness and humanistic learning that kept the *adventus* alive among pageant-devisers throughout mid-sixteenth-century Europe.

Of course not everyone would have understood the elaborate allegories the pageants sometimes presented, which were probably more satisfying to the devisers than to the watchers. Thomas Dekker complained in 1604 that he couldn't identify the allegorical figures decorating the Italian arches in James I's entry, an event for which he himself was the principal pageant-master.[24] But whatever their private thoughts, most people gave public assent to the communicating power of allegory. Preachers and statesmen, scientists and artists, wives and daughters, masters and apprentices regarded the cosmos as a series of great similitudes, each one mirroring all the others. The harmonious and hierarchical relationship between macrocosm and microcosm infused not only their ways of seeing, but also their political and social relationships, as Mulcaster himself took for granted when he later wrote in *The Elementarie* (1582) that 'Her majesty representeth the personage of the whole land.'[25] Mulcaster perhaps believed this more literally than some of the civic politicians for whom he was writing in 1559.

Despite general confidence in the principle of order, the practical details of royal entries were far from rigid and unchanging, and could be easily adapted to local needs and practices. Much depended on who had gained control of the ceremony: the city being entered, or the court of the monarch. In France and Belgium the entry developed as a ritual in which the civic leaders presented themselves to the ruler to invite his confirmation of the rights and privileges of the city's institutions, and the ruler in turn swore an oath to respect them.[26] In England, however, where towns often

---

MacCormack, *Art and Ceremony in Late Antiquity*, 11; for the continuity in visual symbols between triumph and civic entry see Katzenellenbogen, *Allegories of the Virtues and Vices in Medieval Art*, 5–6.

[22]For a more detailed typology, see Bertelli, *The King's Body*, 71–72 and following.

[23]See Robertson, 'L'entrée de Charles quint à Londres, en 1522,' 173–174.

[24]Parry, *The Golden Age Restor'd*, 9.

[25]Mulcaster, *The first part of the elementarie*, *ii^r (modernized).

[26]See Bryant, 'Configurations of the Community in Late Medieval Spectacles,' 13; for the example of Antwerp, see Bochius, *The Ceremonial Entry of Ernst, Archduke of Austria*, vii.

did not have charters and were more likely to invoke the feudal ideal of 'good lordship' for protection, it was the near-sacral status of the king that ensured that lordship.[27] There the ritual discourse engaged in by town and monarch centred not on confirming the identity and rights of individual civic institutions (though that too occurred) but on the display of allegorical representations that communicated this sacral relationship, in particular the relationship between the current ruler and his Biblical antecedents.

For example, in 1486 the citizens of York had to act quickly to secure their position when their patron, Richard III, was defeated by Henry VII. On his entry into the town the new king (who had magnanimously signified he would not accept the usual present of money) met with a series of pageants in one of which the biblical King David greeted Henry as the most 'prepotent Prince in Christendom' and presented him with his 'Swerde of Victory.' The prevailing typological method of interpreting scripture, which imagined the modern king as the fulfillment of his biblical forerunner, thus linked the Tudor monarch to a powerful Old Testament image of his rule.[28]

Of course no one was ever really certain how the ruler would respond. The boy king Edward VI passed rapidly by a speech being delivered at the Standard in Cheapside and a Latin oration at the Little Conduit, but stopped to laugh heartily at a Spanish tightrope walker tumbling on a cable stretched from the steeple of St. Paul's, and in 1604 James I ignored the pageants entirely. The important thing was the enactment itself, during which by showing himself to the people, attending to their presentation of themselves in song, verse and pageant, and receiving their gift with whatever grace he could muster, the monarch confirmed the bond between city and ruler.

London Civic Processions

The apparent timelessness of the ritual is belied by the everyday work many people put in to make the event possible: the circle of political advisors around the Queen, the aldermen who specified which guildsmen

---

[27] See Attreed, 'The Politics of Welcome: Ceremonies and Constitutional Development in Later Medieval English Towns.'

[28] For Henry VII in York, see *York*, I, 146–152, and Anglo, *Spectacle, Pageantry, and Early Tudor Policy*, 27. Typological imagery could be tough-minded: the Florentine pageant at Queen Mary's entry figured her as both Judith and Tomyris, heroines who had decapitated their enemies just as Mary had recently decapitated Northumberland (Anglo, 320–321). For an introduction to typological reading see Charity, *Events and their Afterlife*. For typological readings of kingship in the Tudor period, see especially King, *Tudor Royal Iconography*, chapter 2, 'The Sword and the Book,' 54–115, and *passim*.

were to develop individual pageants, the artificers who built them, the court functionaries who loaned costumes, the painters of mottoes, the singing children, the scenarists and script-writer, and the compositors who typeset the pamphlet. If the entry was, for them, an exceptional moment, the labour that made it possible was also a part of their everyday life, including life's reversals. During the planning of Elizabeth's entry the Painters* 'did utterly refuse to new paint and trim the Great Conduit in Cheap against the Queen's Majesty's coming to her coronation.' The aldermen had to improvise a solution, ordering it to be covered with tapestries and heraldic devices (122).

The citizens had a good deal of experience in staging such events. In medieval York, Chester and Coventry, pageant cycles in dramatic form told and re-told biblical history. In London, where the severe morality of the Lollards was influential, civic and scriptural drama had not flourished, but there was a growing late-medieval audience for travelling players, and religious dramas by the city clerks found a home in Southwark. The first evidence of civic pageantry in England may be that for the entry of the Emperor Otto into London in 1207.[29] The ride from the Tower to Westminster was first described in 1377.[30] In the fourteenth century Chaucer's Cheapside apprentice Perkyn Revelour would dash out of his shop to follow every procession, and then dance till dawn (*The Cook's Tale*, 13–16); Perkyn's descendants would have witnessed the grand processions of the Midsummer Watch, shortly to be absorbed into the inaugural ceremonies for the Lord Mayor.[31] There was genial mockery too; in January 1552 the diarist Henry Machyn, who would also record Elizabeth's entry (101) noted the elaborate 'arrival' from Greenwich of 'the king's lord of misrule' with his attendant young knights and gentlemen, all wearing yellow and green sword-belts; a great scaffold for their merriment was erected at the cross in Cheapside.[32] Machyn reported in

---

[29] For the documents of London drama in the medieval period see I. Lancashire, *Dramatic Texts and Records of Britain: A Chronological Topography to 1558*, xiii–xxiii and passim; Otto's entry is item 880, 173. Withington argues that the first pageantry appeared at the entry of Eleanor of Provence in 1236; see 'The Early "Royal-Entry"' *PMLA* 32 (December, 1917), 617.

[30] Schramm, *A History of the English Coronation*, 94.

[31] For the Midsummer Watch and the Lord Mayor's procession, see Robertson and Gordon, eds., 'A Calendar of Dramatic Records in the Books of the Livery Companies of London 1485–1640,' xiii–xlvi. See also Lindenbaum, 'Ceremony and Oligarchy: The London Midsummer Watch,' and A.Lancashire, 'Continuing Civic Ceremonies of 1530s London.' A procession at the autumn inauguration of London's Lord Mayor is still held today as it has been for nearly 700 years. For the modern show, one of the world's really great parades, see its web site: <http://www.lord-mayorsshow.org/> and figures 5a and 5b.

[32] Machyn, *Diary*, 13–14. Londoners were not the only ones to exploit the public

1553 that in the Lord Mayor's procession had marched 'the crafts of London in their best livery with trumpets blowing...then came a devil and after came the bachelors all in livery and scarlet hoods, and then came the pageant of St. John the Baptist gorgeously with goodly speeches....'[33] Some of those watching Elizabeth's entry could remember at least four other such processions: that of Anne Boleyn (1533), Edward VI (1547), and two by Queen Mary, first upon her accession in 1553 and then the joint entry with her new husband, Philip of Spain in 1554.[34]

It was in these years that London citizens acquired the stagecraft to assemble a royal entry with rapidity. In 1522 Wolsey complained he needed more time to assemble a welcome for the Emperor Charles V,[35] but Anne Boleyn's extraordinary entry, in contriving which the court also played a major role, took just two weeks to prepare, and Edward VI entered the City only three weeks after his accession. Experienced pageant devisers were thus not difficult to find among the informal networks that connected the elites of City and court. Such connections typify the career of the firmly Protestant Richard Grafton, who had not only been King's Printer to Edward VI, and since at least 1548 a close working associate of the new Queen's secretary, William Cecil,[36] but was a recent Warden of the powerful Grocers' Company, and Treasurer-General of the Royal Hospitals. Grafton had helped to prepare Mary's entry of 1554, and he would also supervise Elizabeth's.

Entry and Coronation

The secular royal entry London accorded the new Queen in 1559 thus had a long and well-understood tradition behind it. However, it was only the third section of a greater ritual, that of the coronation. For Elizabeth's, the most propitious date would be established in consultation with Dr. John Dee, the learned astrologer.[37] The details of crowning an English

---

spaces of their city for mockery; see Ingersoll, 'The Possesso, the Via Papale, and the Stigma of Pope Joan' for the ambiguous status of Rome's Via Papale.

[33]Machyn, *Diary*, 72–73. This was only the land portion of the Lord Mayor's procession, which in early days took place partly on the Thames, a splendid location often used for ceremonial display.

[34]Henry's later wives were apparently not accorded formal entries; see Anglo, *Spectacle Pageantry, and Early Tudor Policy*, 277.

[35]Robertson, 'L'entrée de Charles quint à Londres, en 1522,' 169.

[36]For Grafton's various careers, see DNB; also Kingdon, *Richard Grafton*, 78 and passim., and Sisson, 'Grafton and the London Grey Friars.' For Grafton's association with Cecil on Somerset's 1548 commission to study the union of the crowns of England and Scotland, see Hoak, 'The Coronations of Edward VI, Mary I, and Elizabeth I.'

[37]Sherman, *John Dee: The Politics of Reading and Writing in the English Renaissance*, 7.

monarch had been codified in a series of fourteenth and fifteenth-century court manuals.[38] Practices over time varied, but by the mid-sixteenth century, four days were prescribed for the event, each with its separate ritual. On the first day, the monarch travelled by water to the Tower of London. On the second day, in the Tower, he created various followers Knights of the Bath, a lengthy ceremony which included a literal bath. For the third day, that of the entry, the fifteenth-century *Forma et modus* prescribed, 'First of all the prince that is new to be crowned appears before the day of his coronation in noble and fitting array, riding bareheaded from the Tower of London to the royal palace at Westminster, through the city of London. The lords temporal and the commonality of the said city, with the lords and others, are to ride with the King.'[39] On the fourth day, a Sunday, the new monarch was crowned at Westminster, after which there followed a state banquet, where many hereditary functions – eagerly competed for by his attendant nobles – were carried out. Throughout London there were pageants and shows for a week or more during a coronation.

It was not by chance that the secular ritual of a royal entry was scheduled on the day before the sacred ritual of coronation, for during it the monarch was in what anthropologists call a 'liminal' or threshold condition.[40] As she moved from the fastness of the Tower of London into the streets of the City, Elizabeth would begin to leave behind – ritually speaking – the status of monarch-in-waiting she had occupied since her accession.[41] During her passage through the City she would be prepared for her anointing on the next day by offering herself to the citizens for their acknowledgement and accepting their purse of gold, and when she left them behind at Temple Bar she would be integrated into the community as recognized, if still uncrowned, sovereign. Elizabethans would not have conceptualized their customs in this way, but such 'rites of passage' are widespread in all cultures and societies; in our day they are easily recognizable in the first-year initiation customs by which high school seniors are transformed into college freshmen.[42] In a society that had undergone wracking

---

[38] For these manuals, the *Liber regalis* (ca. 1375) the *Forma et modus* (early fifteenth century?) and the *Little Device* (ca. 1483), see Legg, *English Coronation Records*.

[39] Legg, *English Coronation Records*, 182.

[40] On liminality, see Turner, *The Ritual Process: Structure and Anti-structure*.

[41] The difference between uncrowned and crowned king is important even today. Though the abdication of Edward VIII in 1936 was a shock to the monarchy, it was easier to deal with because he had not yet been anointed.

[42] For the anthropology of rites of passage, see van Gennep's classic *The Rites of Passage*.

transformation in recent years, public rituals demonstrating social cohesion were of some importance.

Religion, Politics, and Gender at the Accession of Elizabeth

At least one source of the confidence Elizabeth displayed in 1559 may have been the fact that this was not her first royal entry, but in a manner of speaking, her third. She had accompanied Mary in her 1553 procession, and when Anne Boleyn entered London on May 31,1533, Elizabeth – born only three months later – had in a sense been present as well, though at the time everyone was sure that Anne's visible pregnancy would lead to Henry VIII's long-desired male heir. It did not, however, and consequently Elizabeth's political position at her accession was perilous. As the chronicler John Stow recalled, 'the English nation was wonderfully divided in opinions, as well in matters of ecclesiastical government as in divers points of religion, by reason of three changes within the compass of twelve years.'[43] Well within the memory of those over forty, England had been devoutly Catholic, following the same religious observances as the continental nations from which the crown drew consorts for its princes and princesses, and theoretically subject, in an age when church and state were hardly separable, to the papacy. But in 1534 England had broken away from Rome during Henry VIII's divorce from Katherine of Aragon, set in motion so the king could marry Elizabeth's mother Anne Boleyn, herself a supporter of the new evangelical religion of continental Protestantism. Despite the old king's swings of temper, the men personally closest to Henry VIII in his last years had been firmly reform-minded, and it was this 'evangelical establishment' – Somerset, Northumberland, Cranmer, Ridley and others – who dominated theology and politics during the brief reign of Edward VI (1547–1553).[44] Their insistence on returning to a strictly biblical Christianity would shape Tudor politics, iconography, and literary imagery throughout the latter half of the sixteenth century.

These rapid religious changes were complicated by still-fermenting dynastic rivalries during the brief struggle for the crown when Mary succeeded Edward in 1553. Northumberland failed in his attempt to assert the right to the throne of his daughter-in-law, Lady Jane Grey, and Mary sent both the ambitious nobleman and the unfortunate seventeen-year-old to the scaffold, imposing Catholicism on her people once more. She burned at the stake nearly 300 'Marian martyrs,' the example of whose sufferings, as depicted in John Foxe's *Acts and Monuments* (1563, universally known as *Foxe's Book of Martyrs*) would fuel anti-Catholic

---

[43]Stow, *The Annales, or Generall Chronicle of England*, 635 (modernized).
[44]MacCulloch, *Tudor Church Militant*, 8.

rhetoric in England for centuries. 'Bloody Mary' would go on to marry dangerously – the staunchly Catholic Habsburg prince who was to become Philip II of Spain – and then, after two false pregnancies, fail to produce an heir. A painting of the period depicts the image Elizabethans would later fashion of Mary; in 'The Allegory of the Tudor Succession: the Family of Henry VIII' Elizabeth is depicted accompanied by Peace and Plenty, Mary chained to Philip II and followed by War (see figure 3). Only on her deathbed did Mary give in to pressure to name as her successor Elizabeth, daughter of the hated Anne Boleyn who had displaced her mother, Katherine of Aragon. As she did so, she appealed to her half-sister to maintain the Catholic religion.

The question of which religion the new English Queen would support – and enforce – was of international significance, since Elizabeth's choice could unbalance delicate relationships between the great European powers – the papacy, France, Spain, the Habsburg empire – at a time of immense religious transformation. The political elite around the new Queen, like that surrounding Edward VI, was reform-minded. Anne Boleyn had been a strong supporter of reform, and her daughter, the product of a Reformation education at the hands of Queen Catherine Parr and the circle of evangelically minded Cambridge humanists she patronized, among them John Cheke and Roger Ascham,[45] was known to favour a conservatively reformed – and English – church. The English were also a very nationalist people, proud of the fact that after 1533 Henry VIII's 'imperial' stance united king and people in a single sovereign nation that owed fealty to no higher earthly power.[46] The same unity would be symbolized in Elizabeth's entry by the 'crown imperial,' the familiar closed crown with intersecting arches (see cover), worn by figures representing Henry VIII in the first pageant and the new Queen in the second. This sturdy independence appealed to a broad sector of the public that disliked continental alliances and had been repelled by Mary's allegiance to the papacy and the repressive violence of the early years of her reign. However, the religious question would take time to settle; the rapid transformation of England into a Protestant nation was proving deeply troubling to many who did not want to see the old usages pass away.[47] At Christmas Elizabeth ordered that the English liturgy be used at Mass in her private chapel, and that the host should not be elevated (elevation was a Catholic practice), but it was not until April 1559 that her first parliament chose a moderate path between Catholic and Reformed

---

[45] For the Cambridge evangelical circle see Hoak, 'A Tudor Deborah?' 74n6.
[46] See Hoak, 'The Iconography of the Crown Imperial' and King, 'The Royal Image, 1535–1603.'
[47] See Duffy, *The Stripping of the Altars.*

Figure 3: 'Allegory of the Tudor Succession (The Family of Henry VIII).' Artist unknown. Possibly after Lucas de Heere (1534–1584); ca. 1590. In the centre, Henry VIII hands the sword of justice to Edward VI. On the right Queen Elizabeth leads Peace by the hand, followed by Plenty with her armload of flowers. On the left is Queen Mary, chained to Philip II of Spain, and followed by War. Yale Centre for British Art, Paul Mellon Collection, B1974.3.7.

religion, replacing the Latin liturgy with the Book of Common Prayer but retaining episcopacy as a system of church government. The entry and coronation – the secular welcome and the religious rite – thus had to take place in the uneasy transition period between the Queen's accession and the debating in parliament of the two acts – of Uniformity and of Supremacy – that would later be termed 'the Elizabethan settlement.'[48]

A second major issue was that of the succession; England had had a boy king and an infertile female queen; now it was to have another woman ruler. The fiercest competition between dynastic claimants to the crown had been settled by act of parliament when Mary ascended to the throne over the body of Jane Grey. Ignoring the plans of the dying king

---

[48] For the difficulties encountered in getting the two acts through parliament, see MacCaffrey, *Elizabeth I*, Chapter 5, 'The Religious Settlement,' and more recently Christopher Haigh, *Elizabeth I*, 34–36 and Bowers, 'The Chapel Royal, the First Elizabethan Prayer Book, and Elizabeth's Settlement of Religion, 1559.'

Edward VI[49] she was confirmed as queen on the basis of Henry VIII's third succession act and his subsequent will, an event that manifested the well-established English preference for blood inheritance over inheritance by conquest.[50] However, though a female monarch (as parliament confirmed in 1554) ruled with all the powers of a male monarch,[51] being female she would and indeed should marry so as to produce the essential heir to the throne. Consequently her husband, undoubtedly a foreign prince, would – in view of what everyone agreed was the 'natural' mastery of man over woman – be competing for authority in the realm. As Judith M. Richards observes, 'The best that could be said for a female monarch, either married or unmarried, was that she would be preferable to the even more fearsome alternatives of disobedience to God's providence: usurpation and disruption of the customary practice of the English laws of inheritance.'[52] In 1559 the issue went beyond the fate of Elizabeth's own person, since despite their various dynastic and statutory claims, all those in the immediate line of succession to the new Queen were women as well: Lady Catherine Grey (sister to Jane), Mary Queen of Scots, and Lady Margaret Douglas, Countess of Lennox.[53] What if the Queen were to die suddenly? Historians have recently argued that in 1563 Cecil actually laid plans for temporary rule by the Council in such an eventuality.[54] Not surprisingly, on assembling early in 1559 Elizabeth's first parliament promptly petitioned her to marry, a request she graciously but firmly refused.

The Queen's gender also presented a challenge to the organizers of the entries of both Mary and Elizabeth, for the customary ritual was designed to display a male monarch who was a fighting leader, resplendent in his military *virtù*. A reigning queen – and moreover an unmarried one – would be a single woman among powerful men, and no matter how intelligent and well-prepared, she would surely be a victim of the uncertain emotions that medieval and early modern psychology imputed to women, and which might dangerously destabilize the realm.[55] How

---

[49]See MacCulloch, *Tudor Church Militant*, 39–40, for Edward's urgent attempt in the weeks before his death to obstruct a Catholic succession.

[50]On the political circumstances surrounding Mary's accession, see Loades, *The Reign of Mary Tudor*, 11–17.

[51]For the constitutional issues surrounding the full powers of a female monarch see Richards, 'Mary Tudor as "Sole Quene",' 902–905.

[52]Richards, '"To Promote a Woman to Beare Rule",' 121.

[53]On the line of succession, see MacCaffrey, *Elizabeth I*, 70–71.

[54]See Alford, *The Early Elizabethan Polity*, 110–114 and following, which reproduces Cecil's draft plan (225–228), and for the political setting, Collinson's classic 'The Monarchical Republic of Queen Elizabeth I,' esp. 111–115, 119.

[55]For this kind of theorizing and the view that resistance to it had the paradoxical effect of broadening membership in the political nation, see McLaren, *Political*

then were they to articulate the difference between the status of a queen consort and the more problematic role of a queen reigning in her own right?[56] From medieval times, a clear distinction had been made between the coronation entries of kings and the queens who were their wives. Whereas the King was the central actor in his entry, the queen, however much honoured, played a supporting role.

Nevertheless a queen consort had her own very different authority from that of a male monarch.[57] Her accepted role as mediator between king and people was not just a matter of ideology; medieval queens constantly intervened to advance causes they favoured and to mitigate the harshness of their spouses.[58] And though she might be a lesser being from the philosophical and medical point of view, she was above all a queen, and reigned with her husband's authority when he was absent about his business. That business was usually military, and Renaissance entries stressed the heroic *virtù* of princes whose authority was still defined by their prowess in battle.[59] A queen consort, in contrast, was characterized by her chastity, generously defined as her capacity to produce offspring to inherit the kingdom. Whereas the king made his entry on horseback surrounded by his nobles, the queen consort travelled in a litter beneath a canopy, her long hair hanging down in the manner of a maiden and with her ladies following.[60] The difference in representations could not be more obvious.

The solution was to draw on the iconography of the queen consort, but to re-situate her in the procession as ruler. Though both Mary and Elizabeth travelled during their entries in a litter, not on horseback, their

---

Culture in the Reign of Elizabeth I: Queen and Commonwealth 1558–1585. For an outline of theological and medical views of the physiology and psychology of women before 1600, see in general Maclean, *The Renaissance Notion of Woman*, and on women's emotions, 41.

[56] See Kipling, *Enter the King*, 342–343. Jean Wilson remarks shrewdly on the way queens throughout European history have tried to create public imagery to reconcile their gender and their status – bluestocking Catherine the Great, Victoria as mother of her people, and Elizabeth II as 'the Squire's Lady of the Global Village'; see *Entertainments for Elizabeth* 4–5.

[57] The issue as it affected the accession of England's first regnant Queen, Mary I, is covered in detail in Richards, 'Mary Tudor as "Sole Quene"? Gendering Tudor Monarchy.'

[58] See Parsons, 'Ritual and Symbol in the English Medieval Queenship to 1500,' and his 'The Pregnant Queen as Counsellor and the Medieval Construction of Motherhood.'

[59] The obsession with military *virtù* finally petered out in the eighteenth century; the last British sovereign to command his own troops in battle was George II, against the French at the battle of Dettingen in 1743.

[60] For the significance of allowing the queens' hair to hang loose, see Richards, 'Mary Tudor as "Sole Quene",' 897 and n.11., and 902.

robes were cloth of gold.[61] Both women wore their hair down, a strategy that worked for Mary, whose long hair was reassurance that she intended to marry and hoped to prove fruitful.[62] Elizabeth's entry – at least as far as court display was concerned – followed the general outline of her sister's. She too wore her hair down, and was even garbed in the same gold mantle and kirtle as Mary (depicted in the 'Coronation Portrait' of Elizabeth, see cover and the tailor's account, figure 4 and Appendix II) which as Janet Arnold shows, had been kept and was altered to fit her.[63] But Elizabeth evidently grasped very early that no matter what robes she wore, a literal chastity would have to be central to her authority as a queen regnant. Her unmarried state was to become, for the Virgin Queen, what military *virtù* was for her male predecessors, the mysterious sign and source of her power to rule.

Planning the Queen's Entry

In the face of such issues London's aldermen had every reason to seek stability, and their pride in the traditional customs of London also encouraged continuity – if only for the sake of the crowds who wanted to see yet again their friends the giants Gotmagot the Albion and Corineus the Briton[64] (see figure 5a and Appendix II). But the reciprocity central to all entries positioned the aldermen to promote a special case, and in 1559 that is precisely what they did, by insisting on the relationship between evangelical religion and good governance. Ironically, though the pageant of Deborah would emphasise the sharing of government between the new Queen and her estates, the structure of London's

---

[61] On the differing perceptions of Mary's garb see Richards, 'Mary Tudor as "Sole Quene",' 901–902; see also Arnold, 'The 'Coronation Portrait of Queen Elizabeth I.'

[62] See Richards, 'Mary Tudor as "Sole Quene",' 906.

[63] Arnold, 'The "Coronation" Portrait of Queen Elizabeth I.' There is a slightly shorter account of the same research in her edition of the documents, *Queen Elizabeth's Wardrobe Unlock'd*, which gives a broad picture of Elizabeth's wardrobe over many years.

[64] Gog and Magog are regarded as the traditional guardians of the city of London; inflated plastic figures representing them are still carried in the Lord Mayor's Show today (see figure 5a). They have a complex history, their names in various forms appearing in both European and Arabic sources; see Westrem, 'Against Gog and Magog.' In English national mythology Gotmagot was one of the race of giants wiped out by Brutus and his companion Corineus when, arriving as part of the Trojan diaspora, they conquered Albion. Gotmagot and Corineus, later transformed into Gog and Magog, were condemned to stand guard at the royal palace on the site of the Guildhall, where their carved images (modern ones, because the eighteenth-century ones were destroyed in the Blitz) still rest.

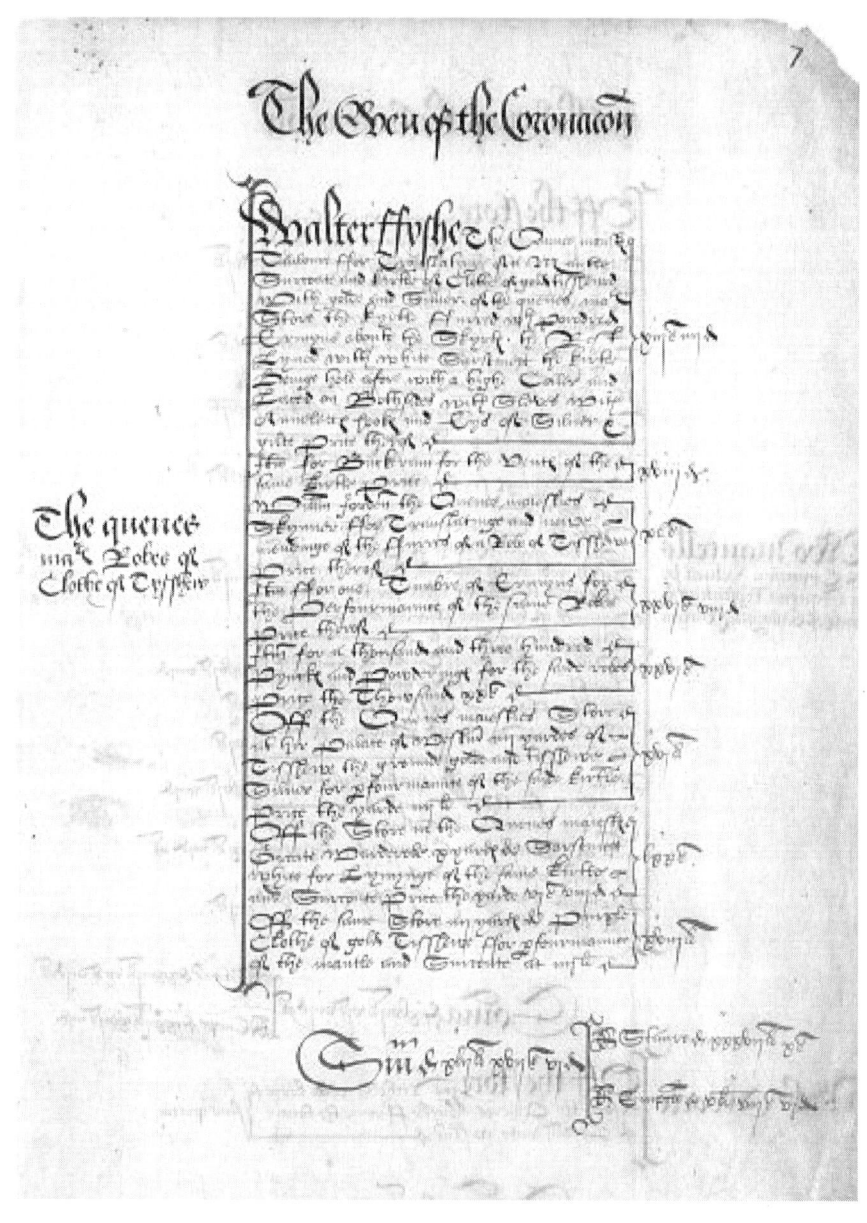

Figure 4: The Lord Chamberlain's record of Walter Fyshe's charges for altering the Queen's dress. The National Archives, London. LC 2/4/3, f.7.

governing body itself was entirely hierarchical. The twenty-six members of the Court of Aldermen, one for each ward, held office for life, and the 212 wealthy members of the Common Council tended to hold their offices for some years.[65] Their design for receiving the Queen was nevertheless determined by their prevailingly radical religion, and given the close links between Richard Grafton, William Cecil, and the evangelicals around Elizabeth, it is likely that no one at court – least of all the Queen — was surprised on the day.

In the accounts of earlier royal entries and processions it is difficult to distinguish between the involvement of crown and of City, though Anne Boleyn's entry in 1533 was certainly managed by the court.[66] Henry VIII interfered several times with the holding of the Midsummer Watch (a clear sign that a public procession had political implications) and after its pageants were absorbed into the newer ceremony of the Lord Mayor's inauguration the aldermen had reason to be wary about future assaults on their privileges.[67] Though no one knows for sure how much Elizabeth's council was involved in framing specific features of the 1559 entry, Cecil's personal memoranda show that he was very busy orchestrating the contributions of court, city, heralds, and clergy to the coronation as a whole.[68] The Queen's brilliant performance during the 1559 procession argues that she must have had some advance knowledge of what was required of her. Cecil's memoranda make it evident she had questioned

---

[65] See Archer, *The Pursuit of Stability: Social Relations in Elizabethan London*, 18–20, and his chapter 'The Framework of Social Relations: The City Elite,' 18–57.

[66] See Ives, *Anne Boleyn*, 218, and forthcoming work by Ágnes Juhász-Ormsby on the propaganda function of the Latin and English verses of Leland and Udall in that entry.

[67] See Lindenbaum, 'Ceremony and Oligarchy: The London Midsummer Watch,' 182. In the event, Elizabeth proved to be less interventionist than her father; see Archer, *The Pursuit of Stability*, 37.

[68] See Hoak, 'The Coronations of Edward VI, Mary I and Elizabeth I,' 120–121. For Cecil's twelve-point memorandum, drawn up on November 17, see Strype, *Annals*, I, pt. 1, 6–7. It testifies to the close interest Elizabeth took in the conduct of that event. Besides securing the Tower of London, closing the ports, and notifying foreign powers and English ambassadors abroad, it notes the need to appoint 'commissioners for the coronation; and the day.' I am indebted for this background to Dale Hoak. On November 18 Sir Nicholas Throckmorton wrote to the Queen saying he had conferred with Cecil 'concerning a proper order for Her Majesty's entry into London'; see *Calendar of State Papers Domestic* I, 115, item 4. This may well refer to her ceremonial journey from Hatfield to the Charterhouse on November 23, described below, but the letter indicates the involvement of the court. Anglo, *Spectacle, Pageantry and Early Tudor Policy*, 14, cites a manuscript account of Henry VII's entry, which was organized 'according to a book made of the order by the king's council,' (modernized).

Figure 5a: Gog and Magog surrounded by the Company of Young Freemen, the Lord Mayor's Show, 2002. Editor.

Figure 5b: The Children of Christ's Hospital in their traditional blue coats, marching in the Lord Mayor's Show, 2002. Editor.

him about the approaching coronation, and it is almost inconceivable that she had not seen at least the 'plat' (scenario) of the entry. But how was that 'plat' worked out?

On December 7 the Court of Aldermen met to assign pageants and displays to various groups of guildsmen, to be set up at the traditional stations: Fenchurch Street, Cornhill, the Standard, the two water conduits in Cheapside, Ludgate and Temple Bar (see figure 6). The central structure of the entry was thus predetermined by the route past processions had taken through the City's public spaces. No effort was to be spared to create a grand occasion; the appointees were requested to ensure that 'all the places hereafter mentioned [would] be very well and seemly trimmed and decked for the honour of the City against the coming of our sovereign lady the Queen's Majesty that now is...as they were trimmed against the coming of our late sovereign lady Queen Mary to her Coronation, and much better if it conveniently may be done' (119). On December 13 four overseers were appointed to supervise preparations: Richard Grafton and Francis Robinson of the Grocers' Company, the Marian exile Richard Hilles of the Merchant Taylors, and Lionel Ducket, a future Lord Mayor, from the powerful Mercers' Company. Not much is known about Robinson, but the other three were, or were to become, men of great influence in City politics.[69] The four were asked to survey the activities of each group, and 'to reform, alter or add unto the same as they with the advice of such as they shall call unto them shall think good' (120). Elizabeth's entry thus grew by a process of controlled accretion: onto a customary processional pattern were grafted the contributions of different groups of citizens, but four overseers had the power to revise what the citizens might suggest, and presumably to contribute themselves.

All this collaborative activity makes it difficult to establish the 'authorship' of *The Queen's Majesty's Passage*, in the sense that word conveys of a single author responsible for the structure and wording of an entire text. A key figure however, is that of Richard Grafton, who had entered public life as the printer (with Edward Whitchurch) of the Bible in English translation (1537) and of Edward Hall's *The Union of the Two Noble and Illustrate Famalies of Lancastre & Yorke* (1548 and 1550).[70] He issued a number of legal books, served as royal printer to Edward VI and was an associate of William Cecil in the late 1540s. He must have been a useful man, since although jailed briefly when he too hastily published Queen Jane's accession proclamation, he shortly returned to favour, and took part

---

[69] For details on all four men see Strong, 'The 1559 Entry Pageants of Elizabeth I,' in *The Tudor and Stuart Monarchy: Pageantry, Painting Iconography*, 38–39.

[70] For Grafton's publications see STC; his successive editions of the Bible in English translation are STC 2066, 2068, 2070–2073, 2075–2076; for his involvement with the complex issuing of Hall, see STC 557.

Figure 6: 7 December 1558: The Court of Aldermen allocates pageant responsibilities. Corporation of London Records Office. Court of Aldermen, *Repertories*, XIV, 1558-1561, ff. 97v-98r.

Thomas Spōn ʒoin'
John hulson ɛrbur
Richard fferror grocer
Wīllm morten carpenter   } for the Condyt in
John Crarkhorne Cutler   } ffletestrete
Lawrence Tavllo Cutler
ffrancis Parker
Edward Loe drap ʒ

George heaton merchaunt ʒ
Wīllm peterson labr   } for ffanchurche
Richard Tavllo grood
Thomas Castell drap ʒ

Henry rayler clotheworker ʒ
George Allen Evans   } for Ludgate
Thomas ricoll goldsmyth
John Lucy Clotheworker ʒ

Wīllm James merchaunt ʒ
Richard Totehill Skevon
Gyles Atkenson merchaunt   } for Temple barre
Bartholmewe brosseby ffrench
Richard brome merchaunt ʒ

in organizing the royal entry of Queen Mary and King Philip in 1554, where his hand may be apparent in at least two pageants exploiting visual imagery from the elaborate frontispieces of books he had published.[71] Grafton rose quickly in the City hierarchy, serving as Treasurer-General of the Royal Hospitals (1553–1555) and Warden of the Grocers' Company (1555–1556);[72] of the four overseers named he was, at the time, much the most powerful. Furthermore, he had a grasp of pageant history; not only had he helped organize the 1554 entry, but in 1542 he had printed one of the several contemporary editions of the chronicle attributed to Robert Fabyan.[73] Fabyan briefly notes whatever reception was given every English king from Henry V onward, and in the edition Grafton printed includes John Lydgate's elaborate verse account of the entry of Henry VI. Lydgate's poem could hardly be bettered as a general model for later pageant devisers, and it had already been ransacked for ideas by the scenarists of Edward VI's hastily assembled entry.[74]

In preparing the entry, it is likely that Grafton and the other overseers would chiefly have functioned as scenarists. Rather than drafting the actual texts of the speeches and verses, they would have determined the organization of the whole and the central devices of specific pageants, for example the display of the Tudor title and of 'worthy governance,' the Beatitudes, the pageants of Time and Truth, and Deborah judging her people. For the verses and mottoes, and for the eventual printed narrative, they apparently turned to a learned young man who was a committed evangelical, recently arrived in London from Oxford.[75] Richard Mulcaster had been educated at Eton and Cambridge, and was expert not only in Latin and Greek, but also in that rare skill even for a humanist, Hebrew. In 1555 he had been accused, justly or unjustly, of stealing money from the influential Cambridge scholar Dr. John Caius, and after a spell in the Tower entered Christ Church, Oxford.[76] His name does not appear on the

---

[71] See Anglo, *Spectacle, Pageantry, and Early Tudor Policy*, 330, 335 and Kingdon, *Richard Grafton*, 63–66.

[72] Kingdon, *Richard Grafton*, 78.

[73] Robert Fabyan, *The Chronicle of Fabyan* (1542). Grafton's edition does not, however, reproduce the detailed account of the procession of Henry VIII that appears in the Guildhall manuscript (Ms. 3313) of Fabyan's chronicle, ed. in 1938 by Thomas and Thornley as *The Great Chronicle of London*.

[74] Anglo, *Spectacle, Pageantry, and Early Tudor Policy*, 283.

[75] Richard DeMolen suggests it was Hilles who brought Mulcaster into the project, having encountered him when both were members of Elizabeth's first parliament; see DeMolen, *Richard Mulcaster*, 8. However, writs for that parliament were only issued on December 5, 1558, and the session did not begin until January 25. In any case Mulcaster, a firm Protestant, would have been naturally drawn towards Grafton's circle when he arrived in London.

[76] For the details of Mulcaster's life see DeMolen, *Richard Mulcaster*, and W.W.

title page of the pamphlet, and indeed when he published an educational treatise, *Positions*, in 1581 he referred to it as the first of his writings to see print. But on March 4, 1559, the Court of Aldermen ordered that 'the Chamberlain shall give unto Richard Mulcaster for his reward for making of the book containing and declaring the histories set forth in and by the City's pageants at the time of the Queen's highness coming through the City to her coronation forty shillings, which book was given unto the Queen's grace' (see page 126, and figure 7). On the continent it was frequent practice for the deviser of an entry to give the monarch a fine manuscript recording the occasion. The presentation of an elegantly decorated book to a ruler involved a degree of formal ceremony that was itself a sign of the giver's fealty and the monarch's recognition of it.[77] Though the printed pamphlet is presented as the narrative of a first person speaker, it is possible that Mulcaster thought of it as a corporate production. However, his firm Protestant views, the passion for order and symmetry in both art and politics demonstrated in his later writings, his limited poetic skills, and his exuberant enthusiasm for any occasion that involved teaching people, all mark the text as his own. Keenly interested in student theatre, Mulcaster was to devise a number of plays and pageants during his subsequent career as a schoolmaster.

Pageant-making was a valuable skill in Renaissance Europe, and the task of publicly displaying the prince's grandeur was often assigned to the trained humanists who were the civil servants of the typical Renaissance court. Such men were devoted to the public use of their considerable erudition; as Mulcaster – himself an educator – would write in his *Positions*, 'What virtue is private?...What learning is for aloneness?'[78] A typical collaboration was that of the teacher and dramatist Nicholas Udall and John Leland, the king's antiquary, who worked together on the extraordinary displays for Anne Boleyn's entry. Leland had died in 1552, and Udall, who left Eton shortly before Mulcaster entered as a student, died in 1556, but there were other experts for a neophyte to consult, not least Grafton himself.[79] Grafton had known Udall, he had close links with the court, his

---

Barker "Richard Mulcaster" in *The Oxford Dictionary of National Biography* (forthcoming).

[77] Inglis, 'A Book in the Hand: Some Late Medieval Accounts of Manuscript Presentations,' 70, and Johns, *The Nature of the Book*, 482.

[78] Mulcaster, *Positions*, 192 (modernized).

[79] Given the disparity in dates, Mulcaster could not have been Udall's student at Eton, as Edgerton states; see his Nicholas Udall, 22–23, 33. This misconception goes back to an article on Mulcaster by 'E.H' (Sir Henry Ellis) in the *Gentleman's Magazine*, 1800. But Grafton must have known Udall well; they both lived in Greyfriars, and Grafton issued Udall's carefully supervised translation of Erasmus's *Adagia*, the *Apophthegmes*, in 1542.

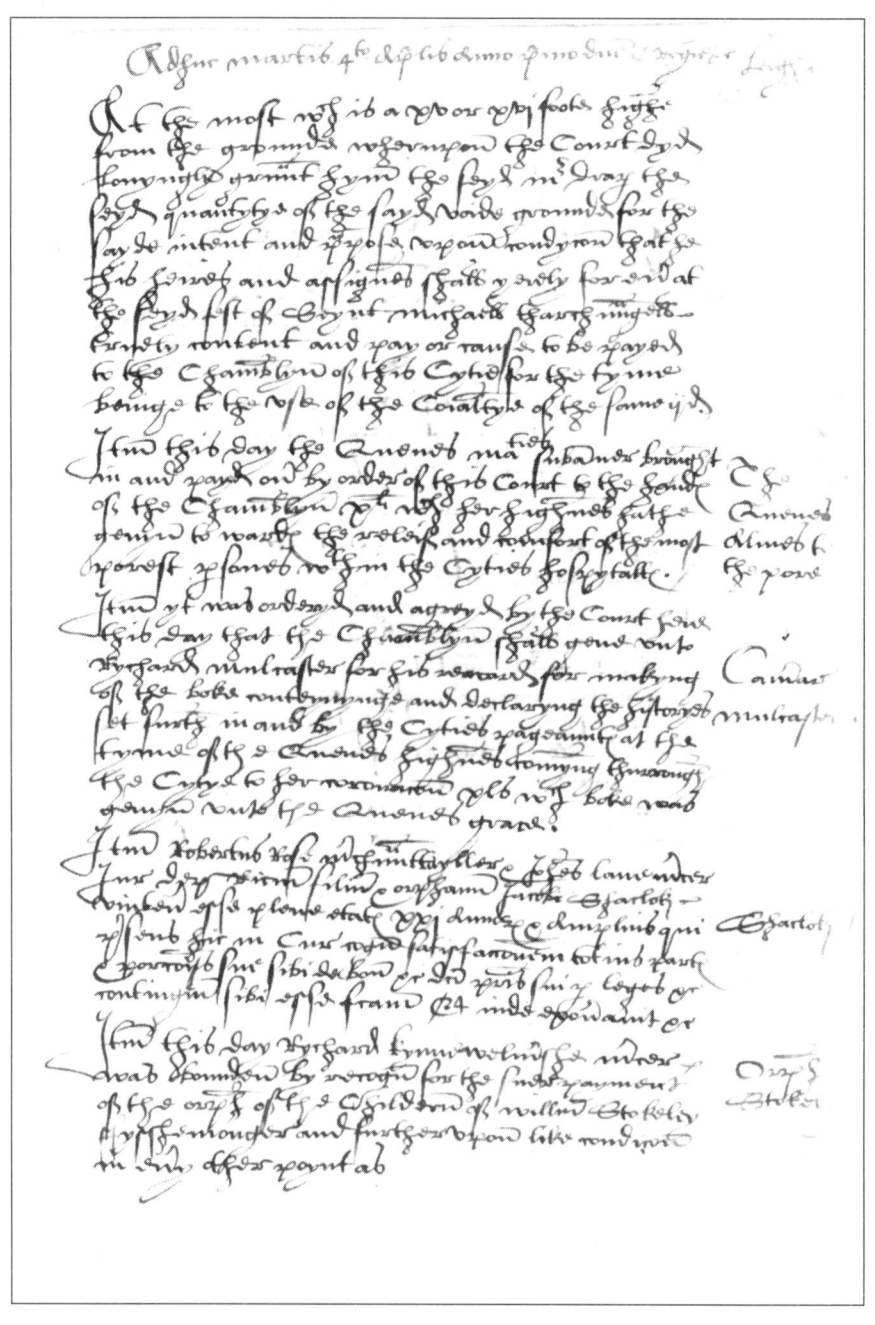

Figure 7: March 4, 1559: The Aldermen receive the Queen's alms for the poor, and pay Richard Mulcaster for 'making of the book'; Corporation of London *Repertories*, XIV, 1558-1561, f. 143^r.

religion was fervently evangelical, he had published the historical sources, and he had the power to 'revise' whatever the guildsmen assigned to an individual pageant proposed. Besides directing the whole, he would have made sure that the genealogical and biblical elements were in place. Mulcaster was an expert Latinist, he too was a committed evangelical, and later in life he would be an enthusiastic proponent of school drama and a frequent contributor to public pageantry. There is, furthermore, a close likeness between the 'unity' emphasised in the pamphlet and the idea of a unified public discourse he puts forward in *Positions* and *The Elementarie*. However the authorship was shared out, it was by these men, during the five and a half weeks between December 7 and January 14, that the 'Receiving of the Queen's Majesty' was designed, written, and mounted. In the meanwhile, Elizabeth and the court were making preparations of their own.

A New Queen Prepares

The eighteenth-century annalist John Strype observed dryly that when Elizabeth was proclaimed Queen 'the bells in all the churches in London rung with joy; and at night bonfires were made, and tables set out in the streets....the satisfaction generally conceived by the people for this new Queen superseded all outward appearances of sorrow for the loss of the old one.'[80] Elizabeth had a seemingly instinctive understanding – no surprise in a daughter of Henry VIII – of the charismatic force, the seemingly supernatural gifts of body and spirit, that Max Weber argued are essential to the domination of a monarch.[81] John Hayward was later to write of her, 'if any person had either the gift or the style to win the hearts of the people, it was this Queen.'[82] Elizabeth was a star, and bitter experience had already shown her how important it was to behave like one. During Mary's reign she had managed her difficult position with wit and resourcefulness. The only event by which she had really been shaken was her 1554 imprisonment in the Tower for alleged complicity in Wyatt's Rebellion.[83] Having escaped the lions' den (an image that would be exploited in the biblical rhetoric of her entry pageant), for four more years she played a demure game of cat and mouse with Mary, acknowledging her half-sister's rule, writing letters of polished regret when it appeared

---

[80]Strype, *Annals of the Reformation,* I ,I, 2. The elites found the London populace unstable; in 1553 the citizens had welcomed Queen Mary's accession just as enthusiastically; see Nichols, ed., *The Chronicle of Queen Jane and of Two Years of Queen Mary,* 11.
[81]Weber, *On Charisma and Institution Building,* 18–27.
[82]Hayward, *Annals of the First Four Years of the Reign of Queen Elizabeth,* 6.
[83]MacCaffrey, *Elizabeth I,* 18.

she might have exceeded her rights, living as modest a life as she could for a woman who was likely to become 'far and away the best marriage to be had in Europe.'[84] But in November 1558 power came into her hands, and as a woman of intelligence, she had not only to grasp it, but to understand its sources. She hinted at how much she had already thought about this when she told the Spanish ambassador, the count of Feria, that it was not the nobility who had placed her where she was, but the people. 'She puts great store by the people,' he reported to Philip II, 'and is very confident that they are all on her side – which is certainly true.'[85]

A 'royal entry' was, of course, a ritual fiction, and Elizabeth made the most of the weeks she actually spent in London before the coronation. On November 23 she left Hatfield Palace* outside London for Sir Edward North's town residence in the Charterhouse,* near Smithfield Market. The historian Raphael Holinshed later commented on 'how comfortable her presence was...to the great multitudes of people that came abroad to see her Grace, showing their rejoicing hearts in countenance and words, with hearty prayers for her Majesty's prosperous estate and preservation.'[86] On November 28 she left the Charterhouse and processed towards the Tower of London, travelling past the City walls and gates in a direction opposite to the one she would later follow on her official entry (see figure 9):

> All the streets she was to pass, even to the Tower, were new gravelled. And so she rode through Barbican and Cripplegate, and along London-wall unto Bishopsgate, and thence up to Leadenhall, and so through Gracechurch Street and Fenchurch Street, turning down Mark Lane into Tower Street, and so to the Tower. Before her rode many gentlemen, knights, and nobles; after them came the trumpeters blowing; then all the heralds in array, my lord mayor holding the queen's sceptre, riding with Garter*; my lord of Pembroke bore the queen's sword. Then came her grace on horseback, apparelled in purple velvet, with a scarf about her neck: the sergeants of arms being about her person. Next after her rode Sir Robert Dudley, (afterwards earl of Leicester), master of her horse:[87] and so the guard with halberds. There was

---

[84] Neale, *Queen Elizabeth*, 76.

[85] Rodriguez-Salgado and Adams, eds., 'The Count of Feria's Dispatch to Philip II of 14 November 1558,' 331. As Schivenoglia's narrative shows (see Appendix I), Feria would eventually march in Elizabeth's entry procession.

[86] Holinshed, *Chronicles of England, Scotland and Ireland*, IV, 156 (modernized). Elizabeth's presence was not quite as comforting to Sir Edward North, who had been sympathetic to the previous regime; he had to leave his house and go to the country.

[87] Despite Elizabeth's close relationship with Dudley, there is nothing unusual about his appearance here; as was customary, Anne Boleyn's litter was also followed by her Master of the Horse; see Pollard, ed., *Tudor Tracts 1532–1588*, 15. The Queen was not amused in 1586–1587 when Dudley, now Earl of Leicester

great shooting of guns, the like was never heard before. In certain places stood children, who made speeches to her as she passed; and in other places was singing and playing with regals.*[88]

To arrive at the Tower in such pomp must have been ironic; it was on Tower Hill that Elizabeth's mother had been beheaded in 1536, and the Tower gate had been the scene of her own fright at being imprisoned in the spring of 1554. But there was craft as well; in making a public arrival in London before her ritual entry Elizabeth was in fact following the example of Mary, who had ridden into London – also on horseback and dressed in purple – on August 3, 1553, accompanied by a vast entourage of nobles and gentlemen. Both these ceremonial processions may have embodied a version of the lustration or 'circuit of the territory' that symbolically cleansed and marked the city for the new reign. The *circuitus murorum* (circuit of the walls) had been known from ancient times, and sometimes occurred during European entries.[89]

On December 5 Elizabeth travelled from the Tower to her London house, Somerset House* in the Strand, 'trumpets sounding, much melody accompanying, and universal expressions of joy among the people.'[90] Queen Mary would be buried in Westminster Abbey on December 14 with all the appropriate dignities, but Elizabeth was making every effort to turn the public eye towards herself, passing from City to Tower to noble residence in a kind of acknowledgement of the political forces in play, before at last arriving on December 23 at the palace of Whitehall, where she spent Christmas. Throughout Christmas week, Strype relates, 'scaffolds began to be made in divers places of the City, for pageants against the day the Queen was to pass through to her Coronation...and the conduits to be new painted and beautified.'[91] On January 3, 1559, Thomas Cawarden, the Queen's Master of the Revels, was given a royal warrant for the loan of costumes from the Revels Office (see page 123 and figure 8).

---

and Elizabeth's commander in the Dutch provinces, was twice given splendid entries of his own 'directly in the tradition of the Burgundian Princes on entering office,' Strong and Van Dorsten, *Leicester's Triumph*, 64; for descriptions, see 43–49, 64–65; see also MacCaffrey, *Elizabeth I*, 225–226.

[88]Strype, *Annals of the Reformation*, I, I, 14–15 (modernized).
[89]Bertelli, *The King's Body*, 75–78. A similar ceremony was – and in places still is – practised locally in England, the ancient practice of 'beating the bounds' of the parish at Rogation-tide (the week before Ascension Day) to ensure everyone is familiar with its limits.
[90]Strype, *Annals of the Reformation*, I, I, 15.
[91]Strype, *Annals of the Reformation*, I, I, 42–43.

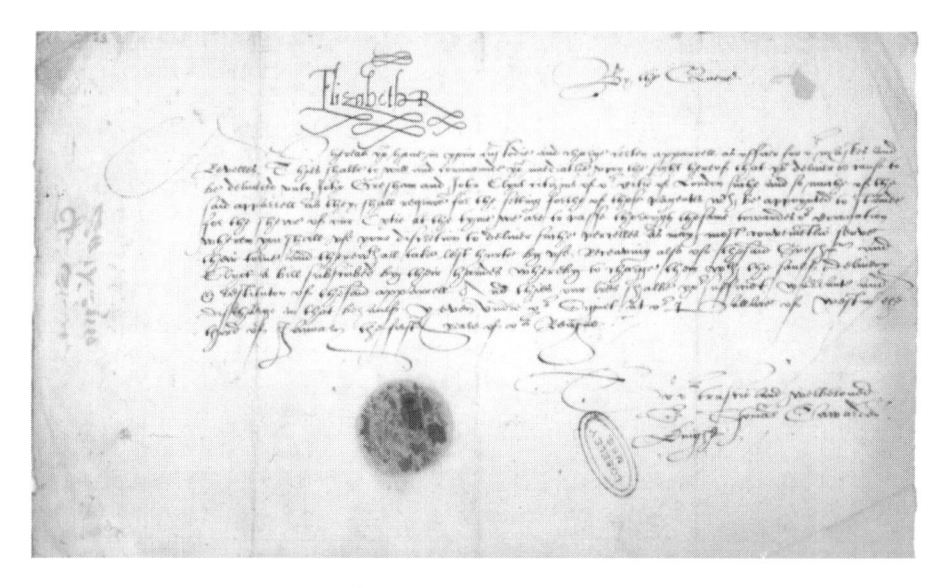

Figure 8: 3 January 1559: The Queen's warrant to Sir Thomas Cawarden, Master of the Revels, for the loan of costumes. By permission of the Folger Shakespeare Library.

'For the Honour of the Said City'

Preparations were also being laid in the City. In choosing Grafton, Robinson, Hilles and Ducket as overseers the aldermen had turned the supervision of the pageant over to representatives of three of the great London livery companies, the Grocers, the Merchant Taylors, and the Mercers.[92] On November 19 the aldermen called a meeting of their Common Council to assess the 'two fifteenths'[93] that would be required to make up the City's gift to the Queen, and to request the wardens of the parish clerks and the City minstrels to 'call severally their whole fellowships together and to put themselves with all convenient speed in good and perfect readiness to do the best and most comely service that they can for the honour of the said City at the Queen's majesty's first coming unto the same' (118). At the same time the two Master Sheriffs of the City were ordered to receive the Queen at the boundary of the shire

---

[92]The 'twelve great' livery companies of London, according to Henry VIII's ranking of them in 1515, were (and still are, as their web sites proclaim) the Mercers, Grocers, Drapers, Fishmongers, Goldsmiths, Skinners, Merchant Taylors, Haberdashers, Salters, Ironmongers, Vintners, and Clothworkers. Members of other companies – the Scriveners, Stationers, Cutlers, Girdlers, Founders and Carpenters – also participated in the 1559 entry.

[93]A 'fifteenth' was a tax on personal property.

Introduction   47

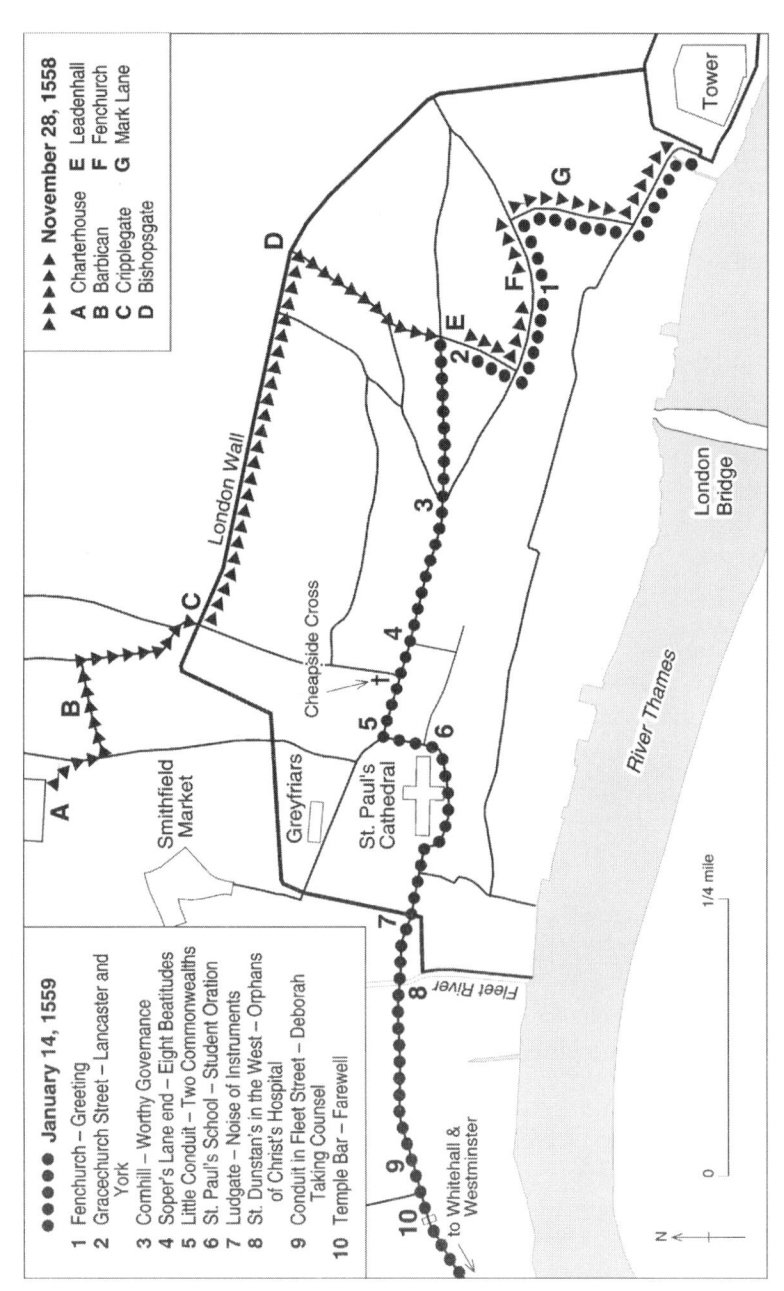

▸▸▸▸ November 28, 1558
A Charterhouse   E Leadenhall
B Barbican   F Fenchurch
C Cripplegate   G Mark Lane
D Bishopsgate

●●●●● January 14, 1559
1 Fenchurch – Greeting
2 Gracechurch Street – Lancaster and York
3 Cornhill – Worthy Governance
4 Soper's Lane end – Eight Beatitudes
5 Little Conduit – Two Commonwealths
6 St. Paul's School – Student Oration
7 Ludgate – Noise of Instruments
8 St. Dunstan's in the West – Orphans of Christ's Hospital
9 Conduit in Fleet Street – Deborah Taking Counsel
10 Temple Bar – Farewell

Figure 9: Map of the processions of November 28, 1558 and January 14, 1559.

48 The Queen's Majesty's Passage

of Middlesex, in their velvet coats and chains of gold, to deliver their rods of office to her and ceremonially receive them back again. On December 7, 1558 the Court allocated responsibilities for specific pageants. As we have seen, 'commoners' (members of the Common Council) were appointed to deck the city for the coming of Elizabeth 'much better if it conveniently may be done' than they had for Queen Mary. This did not prevent them from re-using materials from former pageants, just as three days after Elizabeth's entry the pageants would be taken down 'to serve at another time' (125).[94] We know the names of forty-four merchants and guild members from fifteen different City companies who were charged with preparing individual pageants. And as the instructions to the 'overseers' make plain, the aldermen were ensuring control not only of the general scenario of the entry, but of the monies to be expended; as the procession headed towards the Fleet bridge on January 14, they would make a point of reminding the Queen how much hard cash they had put into welcoming her.

The City of London as Ritual Space

One of the features of a royal entry that pageant devisers sought to take into account was the symbolic geography of the city receiving the ruler. From the beginning of the Christian era, the east from which the Redeemer had emerged was a particularly sacred direction, and churches were built with their altars at the east end. Processional routes, too, moved wherever possible from east to west. The course of the Thames gives the City of London a natural east-west orientation, and the traditional royal entry took advantage of the sacral power of that route. The itinerary began at the Tower of London (see figure 9), where coronation and royal marriage processions had originated since the time of Henry III.[95] In the mid-sixteenth-century London was still enclosed within its ancient walls, long stretches of which various London guilds had repaired at their own cost in the thirteenth century. The Tower was part of those walls; in arriving by water on the first of the four days of coronation festivities, the monarch, in effect, took command of the City's defences. To leave the Tower for the City on the third day was to move from the still semi-rural area of East Smithfield into densely packed urban space; Braun and Haugenberg's 1572 map (based on one of 1553–59, only partly extant),[96] strikingly

---

[94]Alexandra F. Johnston has traced the deployment of one particular pageant castle from 1377 to possibly as late as 1421; see her 'English Civic Ceremony,' 399.
[95]The modern ceremonial route, entirely in Westminster, is familiar from recent royal weddings and funerals; it moves east from Buckingham Palace or St. James's Palace and then south to the Abbey.
[96]Prockter and Taylor, *The A to Z of Elizabethan London*. v.

illustrates the boundary between urban and suburban which would begin to disappear during Elizabeth's reign (see figure 10).[97]

Along the nearly two-mile route from the Tower in the east to Temple Bar in the west, there were three important focal points. The first was the broad expanse of Cheapside, the great market centre of the City proper.[98] At either end of the market or 'cheape' were water conduits, the Great Conduit at the east end and the Little Conduit at the west. A fountain, 'the Standard,' stood near St. Mary-le-Bow, and at Wood Street was the Cheapside Cross, three stories tall and decorated with religious sculptures (see figure 11).[99] In 1559 Perkyn Revelour's descendants would have seen the members of the great City companies standing 'along the streets one by another, enclosed with rails hanged with cloths, and themselves well apparelled with many rich furs and their livery hoods upon their shoulders in comely and seemly manner' (88).

The second focal point was the area around St. Paul's Cathedral. Monarchs occasionally passed into the cathedral to hear a *Te deum*, but this was not a regular practice; they were more likely to find an acrobat performing on the steeple. (If there was such a popular diversion during Elizabeth's entry, the pamphlet soberly does not report it.) The Queen did however hear a Latin oration presented by a scholar of St. Paul's, the famous school founded by John Colet. Finally the procession passed through Ludgate (officially the western boundary of the City) and down Fleet Street, through the increasingly residential area of the lawyers and stationers to Temple Bar. As the procession made its way through the streets, it thus travelled past lanes and alleyways full of the workshops of the various guilds, into the City's most important mercantile space, around the perimeter of its great cathedral, and past the houses and gardens of the new professional classes and the London homes of the nobility, following a route that allowed all the major social units of the citizenry an arena for display, and validating their place in the city as a whole.

If the rich garb of the noblemen signalled the prestige of the court, the staging of the procession itself, dominated by the greater City companies, gave the London guildsmen an opportunity to exhibit to Queen and court the increasing status of the merchant class. The same independence is

---

[97] See Mullaney, 'Towards a Rhetoric of Space in Elizabethan London,' chapter one of his *The Place of the Stage*, esp. 10–19.

[98] Cheapside's importance has not changed in 450 years; see Glossary and Gazetteer.

[99] This was an 'Eleanor Cross'; it had been set up by order of Edward I to commemorate one of the resting places of the body of his wife, Eleanor of Castile (d. 1290) as her funeral procession travelled from Nottinghamshire to Westminster. It was torn down by a Parliamentarian mob on May 2, 1643.

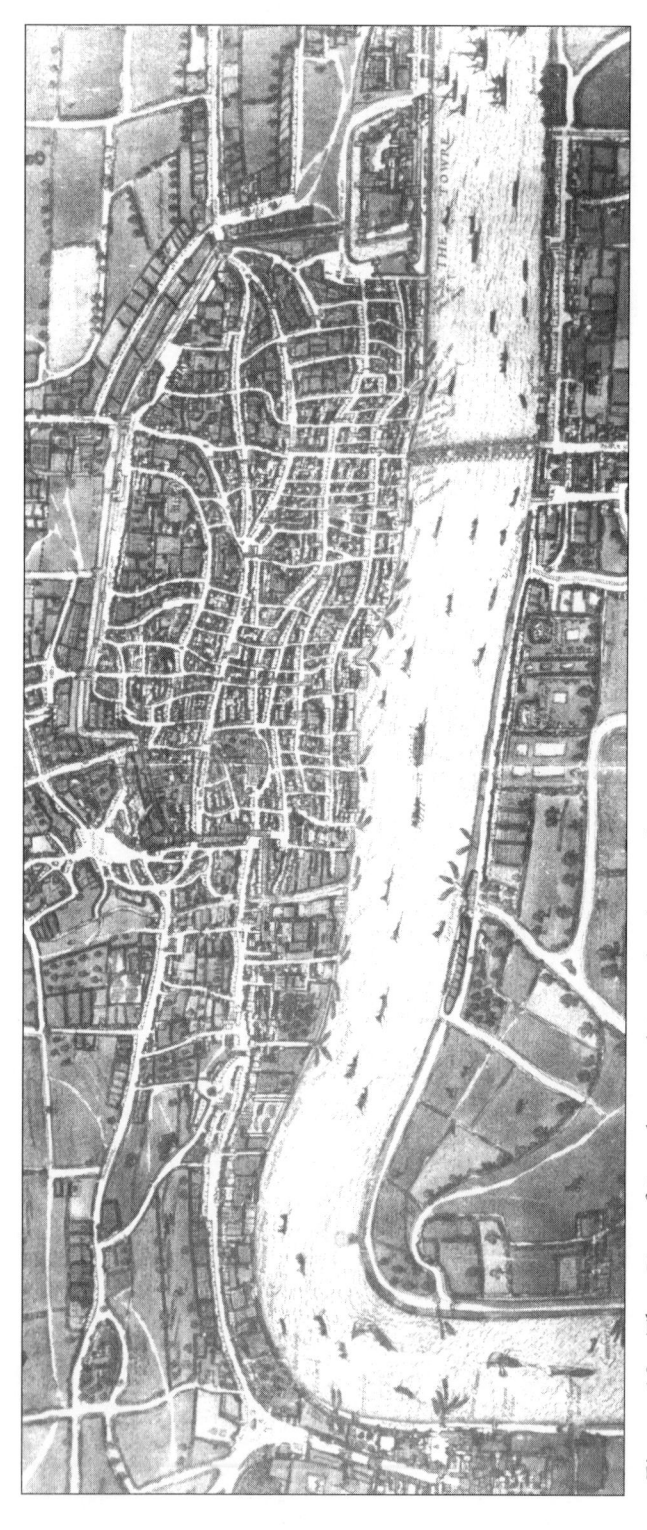

Figure 10: The City of London and its suburbs in the 1550s. Detail of Braun and Hogenberg's 1572 map of London, based on an earlier map made about 1553-59. Montreal: Stewart Museum.

Figure 11: The Cheapside Cross, here with Edward VI passing by during his entry in 1547. Detail from James Basire's 1787 engraving of the now-lost Cowdray House mural of Edward's procession. By permission, the Society of Antiquaries.

evident in an aside levelled at the foreign pageants that had been presented in 1553. European entries often allowed foreign representatives to participate, so as to demonstrate their good will towards the new ruler; in Mary's entry the Florentines and Hanseatic merchants the Queen sought to ingratiate had mounted displays, the Hanse merchants had produced a pageant at Anne Boleyn's entry, and there would be Dutch and Italian pageants at James I's entry in 1604. On this occasion the aldermen would have none of it; as Mulcaster reported, 'the Queen's highness passed through the City, which without any foreign person, of itself beautified itself' (98). Elizabeth's entry was not only to be Protestant, but firmly nationalist, a theme that recurs frequently in the writings of both Grafton and Mulcaster.

Designing the Entry Procession

On January 12, as custom prescribed, Elizabeth travelled by water to the Tower (99) in a scene the Italian observer Schivenoglia compared to the panoply of Ascension Day at Venice, when the famed ceremony of the city's marriage to the sea took place (105). On January 13, she created Knights of the Bath, using English rather than Latin, and omitting such Catholic elements as confession, the all-night vigil, matins (for which the Litany was substituted), and the elevation of the host at mass.[100] And at two p.m. on January 14 she emerged from the Tower, not on horseback, though she had ridden through the City on November 28 and was an excellent horsewoman, but seated in a queen's open litter richly trimmed with gold brocade, and surrounded by footmen in crimson velvet jerkins (see frontispiece). There were over a thousand horses, and the confusion was such that, as Schivenoglia complained, people often lost their places. The courtiers made a superb show, he wrote, and their jewels glittered so much they cleared the snowy air like an alchemist's mirror (106).

Read in isolation, Mulcaster's account of Elizabeth's reception – a rhetorically coherent text with a point of view enthusiastically driven home – leaves the reader with a strong impression that her procession was something unusual. Yet a comparison of the 1559 pageants and displays with earlier ones suggests that the citizens of London got pretty much what they expected to see in the places where they expected to see it. The procession followed the familiar route, there were the usual

---

[100] The ceremonies surrounding making Knights of the Bath have been little noticed in the historiography of Elizabeth's coronation, but there are at least two manuscript accounts, one by Schivenoglia occupying ff. 220^v–223^r of his longer account of the four days of the Coronation (see Textual Note), and another in Bodleian Ms. Ashmole 862, the latter printed by Bayne, 'The Coronation of Queen Elizabeth' (the second of his articles by that name, published in 1910).

painted tables in Latin and English, singing children, Latin orations, triumphal arches, and a frank expression of the hopes of the people, in complimentary but unskilful verse. Yet the question remains: in the framing and performance of Elizabeth's royal entry, who was pulling the strings, and in whose interest? Why was the theme of obedience emphasised so strongly? What were Elizabeth's reasons for apparently assenting to the offering of such forthright advice to one who if only a mere woman, was at the same time an imperial monarch?

Some of these problems are illuminated if we envision the entry as a process, one in which symbol, socio-political advantage, and the personality of the Queen were so closely integrated by the metaphor-seeking mentality of the sixteenth century that they are almost indistinguishable. As with many Renaissance events, the meaning of the Queen's royal entry is as much in the wholeness of its effect as in the words and images of individual parts. To a modern eye, the themes of unity and obedience driven home by the pageants may seem oppressive, as they generally have to feminist analysts of the Queen's seemingly submissive role in the entry.[101] But if we consider the way the ritual itself was used to explore these concerns, we find a more complex response. The spectacle is carefully designed to create a sense of ongoing process as the pageants succeed each other, and there is constant reciprocal action: not only gifts ritually proffered and assurances ritually given, but spontaneous responses by the Queen and apparently by her subjects looking on. It would be easy to assign these features to the pamphlet's attempt to turn the tumult of a public event into persuasive prose, but they are substantiated in the historical example of previous entries, by the practical necessities of staging, in other accounts of the event, by independent testimony as to the Queen's effervescent personality, and by the important role played by ritual exchange in such events.

For the organizers, the challenge of devising a pageant series came from the inevitable tension between the static allegories of the pageants and the linearity of the procession itself, between the pictorial and the expository. The ruler witnessed the pageants in sequence; as Gordon Kipling remarks of the 1501 entry of Katherine of Aragon: 'Katherine [is not] allowed to be a merely passive witness to this drama. She is both audience and protagonist of the show. Indeed, the pageant designer so contrives the Princess's encounters with the pageant actors that she seems to play an active part.'[102] Unlike the Queen, however, individuals in the

---

[101] See for example Frye, *Elizabeth I*, McLaren, *Political Culture in the Reign of Elizabeth I*, Hackett, *Virgin Mother, Maiden Queen*, and Richards, '"To Promote a Woman to Beare Rule"'.
[102] Kipling, ed., *The receyt of the ladie Kateryne*, xv.

crowd could see only what was on display where they were standing in the street. For them, it was necessary to enliven the procession with speeches, songs, and elaborate scenery. In this respect the ordinary citizen was usually well served. However, there is a noticeable difference between processions made up of an amiable hodge-podge of traditional materials, however stunningly displayed, and those like Queen Katherine's, brilliantly devised by an unknown but deeply learned author. Sydney Anglo has termed this 'the most original and complex essay in the pageant medium ever presented in England,' its series of pageants linked together by 'a firm underlying plan.'[103] Indeed as the sixteenth century progressed, ambitious scenarists all over Europe would exploit various ways of linking the separate pageants and displays of an entry together in a unity that was satisfyingly designed and politically instructive. Grafton and Mulcaster clearly took up the challenge; on leaving the City at Temple Bar the Queen was reminded, not for the first time, of the whole purport of her entry by images of Gotmagot the Albion and Corineus the Briton, 'which held in their hands even above the gate a table wherein was written in Latin verses the effect of all the pageants which the City before had erected' (96). 'Unity,' as the pamphlet put it in describing the first pageant, at Gracechurch Street, 'was the end whereat the whole device shot' (81).

Its firm Protestant message aside, that unity emerges from three features typical of the traditional European entry: the exploitation of formal balance in the design of pageants, a stress on reciprocity and exchange, and the assumption that the royal entrant was being instructed in his or her role. First, there was a conscious use of symmetry and parallelism. In entries sometimes hastily assembled by committees, formal balance might consist of little more than familiar elements arranged in paired twos, threes and fours.[104] There are many symmetries in the 1559 entry: at Gracechurch Street two pairs of monarchs and a three-tiered scaffold depicted the Tudor lineage, at Cornhill four virtues each singly trod underfoot two vices (thus illustrating unity conquering division), and at the Great Conduit in Cheapside there was a pageant with three open gates, over the middle of which were three stages on which children representing the eight beatitudes were arranged in a pyramid, 'On the uppermost one child, on the middle three, on the lowest four, each having the proper name of the blessing that they did represent written in a table and placed above their heads' (85–86).

---

[103] Anglo, *Spectacle, Pageantry and Early Tudor Policy*, 8.
[104] For allegorical and typological patterning in a range of European entries, see especially Strong, *Art and Power*, 8–10 and Kipling, *Enter the King*, Chapter I and passim. Anglo notes the degree of symmetrical patterning in the 1501 entry of Katherine of Aragon; see *Spectacle, Pageantry and Early Tudor Policy*, 62–63, and in general 56–97.

Parallelism also distinguished the pageant of the two republics, one ruined and one flourishing, and Deborah in the fifth pageant ruled over 'six personages, two representing the nobility, two the clergy, and two the commonalty' (93). That these symmetries are more than casual is apparent from the careful framing of the entry with a formal welcome at Fenchurch and a farewell at Temple Bar.[105]

The second element is the marked degree of reciprocity and exchange the pamphlet insists on, exemplified not only by the cheers of the populace and the Queen's responses, but the giving of the purse of gold coins at the Little Conduit and the Queen's later acceptance of the Bible in English. Mulcaster's pamphlet has its bias, of course, but genial reciprocity, when it could be achieved, was the aim of every pageant deviser, and even the most indifferent and sullen monarchs had to participate in the material embodiment of ritual exchange, the presentation of the purse or the distribution of largesse. The role of the exchange of gifts in sealing community bonds is well understood.[106] Such exchanges embodied an essential civic language of reciprocal acknowledgement and incorporation. There is both irony and fascination in the fact that if the powerful London merchants were using the opportunity of a royal entry to make clear their conservative political and Reformed religious views, they used the language not of the commodity culture they increasingly represented, but of the sempiternal gift economy shared by societies ranging from the European village to distant and as yet unknown Polynesia. As Louis Adrian Montrose has pointed out, this ritual exchange or 'prestation' is evident not only in the 1559 entry, but also in the constant progresses and entertainments of Elizabeth's subsequent reign.[107]

Thus as the Queen approached Fenchurch Street, probably by coming up Mark Lane,[108] she met with a richly decorated scaffold, with a band of instruments and a child 'in costly apparel which was appointed to

---

[105] There has been some uncertainty about the formal divisions of the 1559 entry. DeMolen, *Richard Mulcaster*, 134, states that there were eleven 'stopping points' during the entry. Susan Frye counts eight 'scenes,' including the 'digression to describe the elaborately staged presentation of the city's purse to the queen' See *Elizabeth I*, 24.

[106] See Mauss, *The Gift: the Form and Reason for Exchange in Archaic Societies*; For the lively Renaissance practice of gift exchange, and an important review of studies of prestation since Mauss, see Davis, *The Gift in Sixteenth-Century France*.

[107] See Montrose, 'Gifts and Reasons: The Contexts of Peele's Araygnment of Paris,' 447–453.

[108] Elizabeth's route from Tower Green and up Mark Lane is speculative, but from Fenchurch Street we know street by street the route of the procession. Edward VI's procession travelled up Mark Lane; see *Literary Remains of King Edward the Sixth*, I, cclxxxi.

welcome the Queen's Majesty in the whole city's behalf' (78).[109] The verses he spoke offered her two gifts:

> The first is blessing tongues, which may a welcome say
> Which pray thou mayst do well, which praise thee to the sky.
> ...
> The second is true hearts, which love thee from their root
> Whose suit is triumph now, and ruleth all the game.

The pamphlet relates that Elizabeth 'of her own will' asked the musicians to stop playing so she could hear the child speak, and it goes on to emphasise the extent to which she listened responsively; 'the words took no less place in her mind than they were most heartily pronounced by the child, as from all the hearts of her most hearty citizens'. At the end of the entry, as Elizabeth departed from Temple Bar, the concluding element of the frame was put in place. Not only was the whole event explained to her in the 'tables' posted above the gate, but again there was music, this time from singing children, and a child – here dressed as a poet – who spoke these lines:

> As at thine entrance first, O prince of high renown,
> Thou wast presented with tongues & hearts for thy fare,
> So now since thou must needs depart out of this town
> This city sendeth thee firm hope and earnest prayer. (97)

Hearing this, the Queen is reported to have held her hands up to heaven and encouraged the people to say Amen. Thus the five great pageants of the entry were formally bracketed by two episodes of gift-giving, explicitly parallelled by the use in both cases of music and of individual child speakers.

Finally, as we have seen, royal entries provided opportunities for counsel; their pageants, tables and allegories displayed the virtues the citizens believed the monarch should possess, and great royal entries like Katherine of Aragon's could present powerful cosmological visions. Grafton's and Mulcaster's did not ascend those heights, but there was an evident exploitation of the sequence of pageants to educate the young Queen in her role. The first pageant was genealogical; *The uniting of the two houses of Lancaster and York*, at the upper end of Gracechurch Street,

---

[109] The question of whether women (who did not appear on the stage) took part in civic pageants is unresolved owing to a lack of evidence one way or the other. However, in the description of Queen Mary's 1553 entry there are several references to children deliberately dressed in girl's or women's apparel, which suggests that they were in fact boys, and therefore that women and girls did not take part; see Nichols, ed., *The Chronicle of Queen Jane and of Two Years of Queen Mary*, 29–30.

explained her title to the crown of England as it descended from Henry VII and his wife, the Queen's namesake, Elizabeth of York. This way of exhibiting the Tudor title as a union of York and Lancastrian dynasties was by no means new,[110] but the prudent inclusion of the executed Anne Boleyn was a marked change from the time not long past when Anne had been a rejected consort and her daughter declared a bastard.

The second pageant was located at the lower end of Cornhill, and illustrated the conflicting forces that a monarch must master to ensure the kind of unity referred to in the 'sentences' or tables (posters) pasted up in the previous pageant. Based at a remote distance on allegorical figures descended from the *Psychomachia* of the Christian Latin poet Prudentius (348–ca. 405), *The seat of worthy governance* showed Pure Religion, Love of Subjects, Wisdom, and Justice treading beneath their feet the contrary vices of Superstition and Ignorance, Rebellion and Insolence, Folly and Vainglory, and Adulation and Bribery, all terms used by Protestant propagandists to signify Catholicism.[111] Above, the arms of England were displayed, upheld by their appropriate heraldic beasts, and a figure depicted Elizabeth, now wearing the closed imperial crown in her own right.

The third pageant, *The eight beatitudes...applied to our sovereign lady Queen Elizabeth* took place at Soper's Lane near the Great Conduit in Cheapside. Drawn from the passage in the Gospel of St. Matthew known as the Beatitudes (Matt. 5, 3–10), it showed what gifts Elizabeth brought to her reign. The blessings that had been bestowed on her were meekness of spirit, 'mourning in thy grief and mildness in thy blame' (alluding to her deportment during her 1554 captivity), her endurance when justice was withheld, her demonstration of mercy despite oppression, her cleanness (that is, purity) of heart, and her search for peace despite persecution.[112] The pageant harks back to, if it does not specifically echo, a moment in the entry pageant of Edward VI, when at the conduit in Fleet Street the figure of Ancient Truth (that is, evangelical Christianity) had told the boy king that if he embraced Truth, 'then shall the God of Truth give you his grace / To bring your devices luckily forward.'[113] The verses

---

[110] Anglo comments on the frequency of the motif in pageantry, literature, art and music throughout the Tudor period; see *Spectacle, Pageantry, and Early Tudor Policy*, 24.

[111] On Prudentius's allegorical figures and their later adaptations, see Katzenellenbogen, *Allegories of the virtues and vices in medieval art;* he stresses the connection between later pictorial versions of these allegories and Roman relief sculpture, especially on triumphal columns (5–6). The inherent contrariness of the vices is signified by the fact that there are two of each.

[112] The somewhat contorted verse the child was required to speak gains slightly in clarity by comparison with a translation of the Latin version (128).

[113] *Literary Remains of King Edward the Sixth*, ccxci.

of this pageant completed the first phase of the Queen's preparation by demonstrating that a gift had been given Elizabeth by God: with the blessings he had bestowed on her she had demonstrated in her endurance under trial how worthy of them she was. Out of this experience had come God's promise to the Queen, based on her demonstrated virtues: 'Therefore trust thou in God, since he hath helped thy smart / That as his promise is, so He will make thee strong' (87).

The Politics of Imagery

The imagery exploited in the first three pageants of the entry is not unexpected; genealogical pageants had appeared in earlier entries,[114] the allegories of *The seat of worthy governance* would have been familiar all over Europe, and the Beatitudes were hardly controversial. But for different reasons the images of the bible, Truth as the daughter of Time, and the prophet Deborah were much more problematic. All would have entertained the groundlings, but the watching elites would have recognized significant religious and political nuances in the way they had been appropriated and re-appropriated by different factions. Grafton and Mulcaster had clearly set out to define their meanings for the new reign. These pageants made clear the firmly evangelical views of the entry's devisers, with which Londoners would have been sympathetic, but they also raise the problem of how much the court – and particularly the Queen's secretary, William Cecil – were able to control its unfolding. Events were also complicated by Elizabeth's reaction to the experience she was undergoing. Mulcaster's pamphlet frequently points out her enthusiasm, and the Queen's habitual spontaneity is independently documented by several observers. Schivenoglia, for example, sniffed that on leaving Westminster Hall after her coronation the next day Elizabeth smiled so much and greeted everyone so warmly that 'for my part she overstepped the limits of decorum and gravity.'[115] A consequence of her intense involvement was that no one could be absolutely certain what the Queen was going to do next. In events at the Little Conduit and afterwards, we witness what may be an on-the-spot reconciliation, one that worked to the advantage of both parties, between the plans of the pageant scenarists and the Queen's improvisatory instincts.

---

[114] See for example Anglo, *Spectacle, Pageantry and Early Tudor Policy*, 335. In James I's 1604 entry, it was the Italians who mounted the genealogical pageant, which showed Henry VII passing the sceptre to James as the true successor to the Tudor line; see Parry, *The Golden Age Restor'd*, 9.

[115] Mantua: Archivio di Stato, Archivio Gonzaga, Schivenoglia to Calandra, January 23, 1558, f. 232^r.

Just as the procession left the Cheapside Cross Elizabeth glimpsed ahead the next pageant, erected at the Little Conduit. Asking what it was about, she was told that 'there was placed Time. "Time," quoth she, "and Time hath brought me hither"' (87). It was at this moment that the Queen briefly attempted to bend 'time' to her service: being told that in this pageant 'the Bible in English'[116] would be delivered unto her by Truth, she commanded Sir John Parrat [or Perrot], one of the knights holding up her canopy, to fetch it to her. However, when it was explained that the Bible was later to be lowered to her on a silken lace, she kept Parrat back and passed on to the aldermen waiting at the high end of the market.[117] Possibly the Queen had simply mistaken what she was supposed to do. If so, why did the pamphlet, with its panegyrical purpose and tone, report such a minor gaffe in such detail? Significantly, this was the pageant that staged the gift to the monarch of *The Byble in Englyshe*, a text central to the evangelicals' programme, and bearing the title of an edition which Grafton himself had published in 1539 (see figure 12). Nothing that involved the bible in this entry could possibly be placed at risk, and the knight dispatched to receive the Bible must have been carefully chosen, probably by the court. Sir John Parrat is one of the few persons specifically named in Mulcaster's text; indeed in the course of printing the pamphlet a special effort was made to ensure he was properly identified.[118]

A bluff, heavy-set man with a reputation as a hell-raiser, Parrat was widely regarded as one of Henry VIII's illegitimate sons; the gossips of court and City would have believed him as closely related in blood to Elizabeth as had been Edward VI and Mary.[119] Despite his early hooligan reputation Parrat was trusted for some years by Elizabeth; he served as vice-admiral of the Welsh seas, President of Munster and – fighting fiercely

---

[116] Grafton published the first Great Bible, described on the title page as *The Byble in Englysshe*, in 1539 (STC 2068); see figure 12.

[117] There has been surprisingly little comment this event, which is not mentioned in any other narrative. See however Frye, *Elizabeth I*, 47, Wilson, *Entertainments for Elizabeth*, 6–7, and Mary Hazard, *Elizabethan Silent Language*, 220, who follows Frye. For two very different interpretations argued at greater length see Logan, 'Making History' and Leahy, 'Propaganda or a Record of Events?'

[118] Care was taken to make sure Parrat's name was printed correctly in the only extant copy of the first edition; on f. Cii^v a slip of paper reading 'John' has been pasted over a typographic error in his name, and in the second 1559 printing 'master Parrat' is given his proper title, 'Sir John' (Ciiii^v). See Textual Note.

[119] Sir John Parrat or Perrot (1527–1592) held various offices under Elizabeth; he 'united great physical strength to a violent and arbitrary disposition' (DNB). The gossip that circulated around his parentage was confirmed in the view of everyone by his close physical resemblance to Henry VIII. Leahy, 'Propaganda or a Record of Events?' regards Parrat's involvement in the presentation of the Bible as scandalous, but the notorious English respect for blood relationships would have guaranteed his position.

Figure 12: Title page of Richard Grafton and Edward Whitchurch's edition of 'The Byble in Englysshe' (London, 1539). By permission of the British Library (C.18.d.1).

and living in great estate – as Lord Deputy of Ireland. Incarcerated in the Tower in 1591 on a trumped-up charge of treason, Parrat is reported to have exclaimed, 'God's death! Will the queen suffer her brother to be offered up a sacrifice to the envy of his frisking adversary?' (DNB). He died in September before judgement was executed on him. A laudatory biography by Parrat's son tactfully omits the rumours of Sir John's parentage, emphasising instead the difficulties he had encountered as a declared Protestant during the Marian period.[120] But whatever people thought of Sir John Parrat when the biography saw light in 1728, in 1559 he seems to have been regarded by everyone (including apparently himself) not only as a son of Henry VIII, but as a Protestant who had stood by his religion. If so, his symbolic capital must have been considerable, and whoever selected him to receive the bible was very shrewd. Describing the Queen's unexpected intervention, Mulcaster may have welcomed the chance to emphasise the link between the union of the Tudor genealogical tree (in the form of the stout person of Sir John) and the Word of God.

It was the union of City and Monarch, however, that featured in the next part of the entry. When Elizabeth finally arrived at the upper or west end of Cheapside, she found Ranulph Cholmley, Recorder* of the City, arrayed with those of the City fathers who were not already taking part in the procession, and ready to present her with 'a purse of crimson satin richly wrought with gold, wherein the City gave to the Queen's Majesty a thousand marks in gold' (88) His speech was brief, declaring 'their gladness and good will towards the Queen's Majesty [and]...desiring her Grace to continue their good and gracious Queen, and not to esteem the value of the gift but the mind of the givers.' The Queen's reply, 'in words truly reported,' the pamphlet emphasises, was to 'thank my lord mayor, his brethren, and you all. And whereas your request is that I should continue your good lady and Queen, be ye ensured that I will be as good unto you as ever Queen was to her people' (88–89). Yet again the emphasis was on reciprocity, not only in the earnest politics of the pamphlet, but in the ancient custom of presenting the gold.

However, politics loomed large in the following pageant, which flaunted the recuperation of a image much exploited by Protestants, but which Mary had attempted to turn into Catholic propaganda. At the Little Conduit outside the church of St. Michael le Querne (see figure 13), Elizabeth encountered a typical sixteenth-century visual allegory. Standing foursquare before the conduit was a battlemented structure, with two hills. The one on the north side, named *Ruinosa respublica* (a decayed commonwealth), was barren and stony. That to the south, *Respublica*

---

[120] Perrott, *The history of that eminent statesman, Sir John Perrott* (1728).

62   The Queen's Majesty's Passage

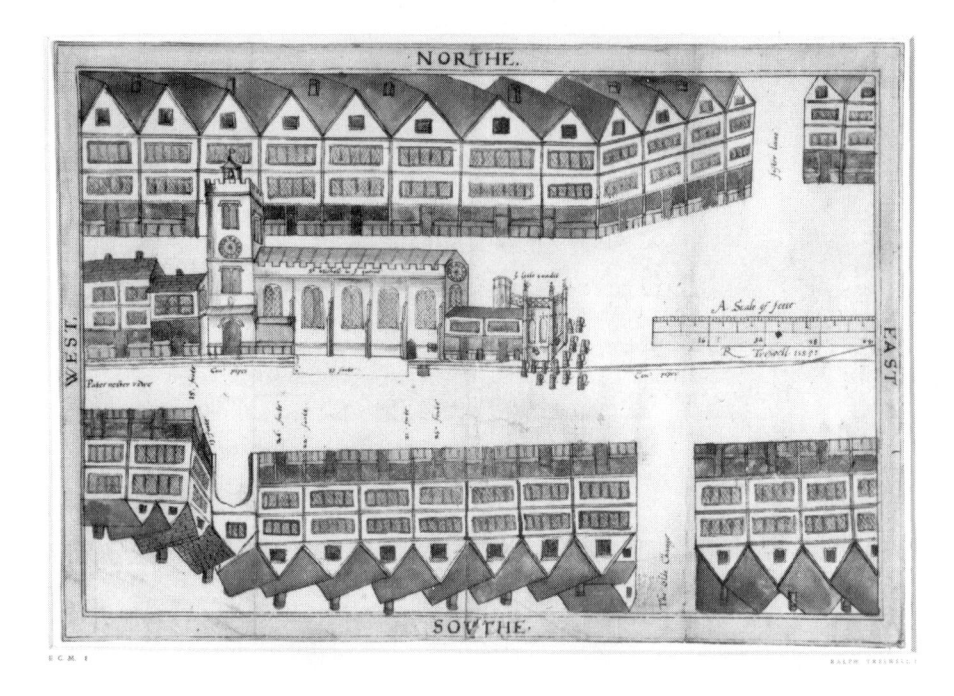

Figure 13: Ralph Treswell's drawing of the church of St. Michael le Querne at the west end of Cheapside (1585), showing the Little Conduit with water-pots standing around it. British Museum, Crace Collection 1880-11- 13-3516. © The British Museum.

bene instituta (a flourishing commonwealth), was fresh and green. Between the two was a cave with a locked door, from which issued as the Queen approached the figure of Time, the familiar old man with a scythe, leading by the hand *Temporis filia*, the daughter of Time, who had a label on her breast naming her as *Veritas* or Truth. In her hand she carried a book 'upon the which was written *Verbum veritatis*, the Word of Truth' (89).

The image of Truth as the daughter of Time had a long ancestry.[121] The proverb circulated widely in Europe, both as a philosophical motif exploited by controversialists during the Reformation's great debate over what constituted theological Truth, and as an image much used by the artists and learned men who had recently invented the popular emblem book, with its combination of symbolic pictures and admoni-

---

[121] For the history of this motif, and a sense of the richness and variety with which it was exploited in sixteenth-century Europe, see Saxl, 'Veritas filia temporis'; King traces its English history in *Tudor Royal Iconography*, 102–103, 189–195.

tory mottos.[122] Perhaps because in England '*Veritas temporis filia*' had furnished an evangelical slogan, the Catholic Queen Mary appropriated the image for use on her personal device, for the legend on her crest, on the Great Seal, and on her coins.[123] Notwithstanding her reworking of the image, '*Veritas temporis filia*' would also appear on the title page of the Marian exile William Whittingham's revision of the New Testament in English (1557) (see figure 14), as well as on the title page of John Knox's *First Blast of the Trumpet Against the Monstruous Regiment of Women* (Geneva, 1558), which argued passionately against female rulers. In the 1559 entry the pageant of Truth and Time thus carried a heavy load of significance. Not only did it restore to the image its recognized evangelical meaning, but displayed in a pageant for a female ruler it also put Knox's *Blast* in its place. Truth had been imprisoned in her rock for many years, and Time, in the form of Elizabeth's accession, had now brought her forth to lower from her hill the book – the Bible in English – that Sir John at last took and delivered to the Queen. 'Elizabeth's kissing and embracing of the bible,' writes John N. King, 'could not have announced her religious sympathies more boldly.'[124]

It is not clear who engineered the dramatic impact of this pageant and the moments that led up to it. The specifically biblical element must have been supplied by Grafton, for the Latin verses attached to this crucial pageant do not mention the Bible at all, a sign perhaps of Mulcaster's humanist purism in adhering to classical (and therefore pre-Christian) example. However, in 1554 Grafton had struggled and failed to assert the relationship between the Tudor dynasty and '*Verbum dei*,' the Word of God. In that year's entry of Mary and Philip, which he helped devise, the pageant at the conduit in Gracechurch Street had pictured the nine worthies and Kings Henry VIII and Edward VI. All bore arms except for Henry, who was painted 'having in one hand a sceptre and in the other hand a book, whereon was written *Verbum dei*.' The painter was called before the Bishop of Winchester, who told him 'it is against the Queen's catholic proceedings' and threatened to throw him in the Fleet prison; he hastily repainted the image with Henry holding a new pair of gloves.[125] It

---

[122] There is an extensive literature on the emblem book, a European phenomenon from the sixteenth century right into the nineteenth; for background, see Manning, 'Emblems.'

[123] Saxl, 'Veritas filia temporis,' 207; for the proverb in Marian England and afterwards, see Gordon, 'Veritas filia temporis: Hadrianus Junius and Geoffrey Whitney.'

[124] King, *Tudor Royal Iconography*, 231.

[125] Nichols, *The Chronicle of Queen Jane and Two Years of Queen Mary*, 78. Nichols notes that 'this passage is crossed out in the MS. as if the writer had been fearful of retaining it.' The same anecdote is related in several other sources.

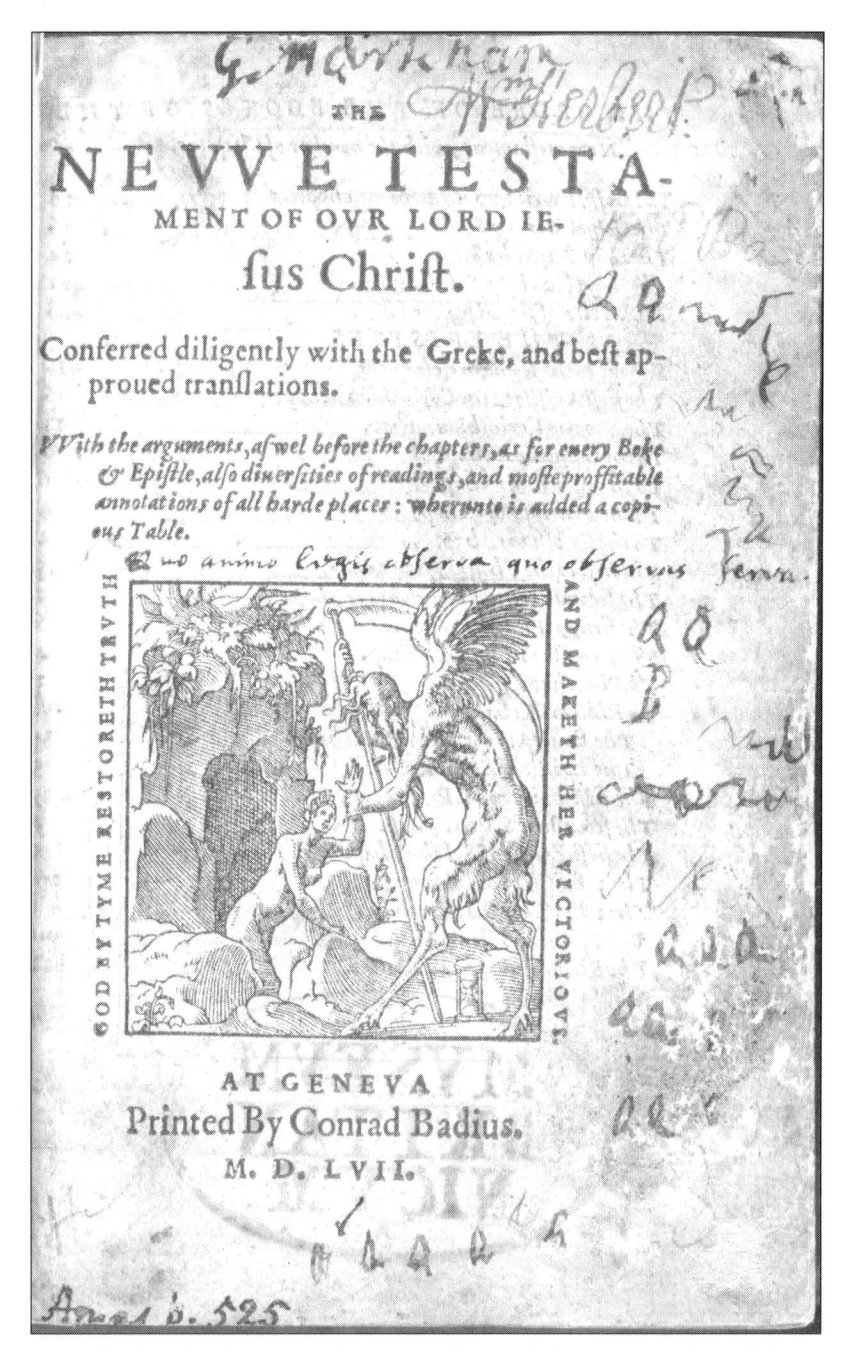

Figure 14: The figures of Time and Truth from the title page of William Whittingham's revision of *The Newe Testament of Our Lord Iesus Christ* (Geneva, 1557). By permission of the British Library (C.17.a.15).

must have given Grafton immense satisfaction to develop the 1559 procession so that the Word of God was now central to its meaning.

At the next display it was Mulcaster's turn; here the future schoolmaster's learning had full play, in the form of a Latin oration spoken by a St. Paul's schoolboy. Like the other Latin sections of the entry the oration is self-consciously classicizing; the daughter of Henry VIII becomes the 'prince' of humanist political thought. Taking its cue from Plato's account of the education of the guardians in *Republic* vii, the Queen is lauded for her gifts both of body and spirit, and for the nobility of mind and learning that ought to characterize the Renaissance ideal of the good ruler. Elizabeth 'shines with the virtues of the British people, and protects them with the shield of justice....At her command, piety shall thrive, England flourish, the golden ages return' (92 and 129). Here we meet with what may be the first suggestion of Elizabeth as an Astraea figure, and probably in the words of the humanist schoolmaster of the author of *The Faerie Queene*.[126]

In general, however, the imagery employed for Elizabeth's entry was historical and biblical, not classical. The fifth and final pageant was located at the water-conduit in Fleet Street, and almost more than any other, it illustrates the way in which the pageant-makers could take an exemplary image and turn it to their special purposes. Based on the sketchy account of Deborah in the fourth and fifth chapter of the book of Judges, it displayed the Israelite prophet beneath her iconic palm tree (Judges 4, 4–5). However, it showed her with an open rather than an imperial crown,[127] and arrayed in 'parliament robes' (93). The pageant thus figured forth not Deborah's saving of the Israelite people so much as her supposed behaviour (not touched on in the Bible) in consulting with her estates for the good government of her people. In its characteristic pedagogic mode the pamphlet informs us, 'The ground of this last pageant was, that forasmuch as the next pageant before had set before her Grace's eyes the flourishing and desolate states of a commonweal, she might by this be put in remembrance to consult for the worthy government of her people, considering God oftimes sent women nobly to rule among men, as Deborah which governed Israel in peace the space of forty years, and that it behooves both men and women, so ruling, to use advice of good counsel' (94–95).[128]

---

[126] Though she does not note this possible early allusion, Yates points out the early connection between the Virgin Queen and the return of the goddess Astraea, and its setting in imperial theorizing; see her *Astraea: the Imperial Theme in the Sixteenth Century*, 29–87, esp. 47.

[127] Deborah may have been shown with a simple open crown because she (unlike Elizabeth) was not an imperial monarch.

[128] For Grafton's two accounts of this pageant, see Appendix I; that of 1570 is slightly fuller, and (whether out of prudence or for some other reason) states that

The Deborah pageant has recently proved a magnet for students of Elizabeth's early politics.[129] Was the daughter of Henry VIII, already a woman of very firm purpose, offended by the suggestion that she ought to rule with the advice of parliament? Two months previously she had impressed the count of Feria as 'determined to be governed by no one.'[130] Yet the concept of shared power had been in the air for a decade; as Stephen Alford points out, 'in the main, Edwardians sketched a collaborative Reformation promoted by a king counselled, endorsed by parliament.'[131] The name of Deborah had been invoked by John Knox in his attack on Mary Queen of Scots, *The First Blast of the Trumpet Against the Monstrous Regiment of Women*, published at Geneva earlier in the year and a subject of discussion among the Marian exiles flocking back to England in December.[132] Knox insisted that a ruling queen was a clear interruption of the order of nature; 'the erecting of a woman to that honour, is not only to invert the order which God hath established, but also it is to defile, pollute and prophane...the throne and seat of God, which he hath sanctified and appointed for man only.'[133] He dismissed the case of Deborah, arguing that 'examples have no strength, when the question is of law.'[134] John Aylmer's prompt response to Knox, *An harborowe for faithfull and trewe subjectes* (1559), would provide a

---

'This was made to encourage the Queen not to fear though she were a woman; for women by the spirit and power of Almighty God have ruled both honourably and politiquely, as did Deborah' (114).

[129] Among studies already cited, see Frye, *Elizabeth I*; McLaren, *Political Culture in the Reign of Elizabeth I*; Hoak, 'A Tudor Deborah?' and Richards, '"To Promote a Woman to Beare Rule".'

[130] Rodriguez-Salgado and Adams, eds., 'The Count of Feria's Dispatch to Philip II', 331.

[131] Alford, *Kingship and Politics in the Reign of Edward VI*, 204; see also Hoak, 'A Tudor Deborah?' 85–86. For the aftermath of this view of Elizabeth in seventeenth-century Parliamentarian political discourse, see Watkins, '"Old Bess in the Ruff."'

[132] Interestingly, the source of the Deborah comparison seems to have been John Calvin himself, who had mentioned her example to Knox in a conversation about 1557. He was furious at Knox's subsequent attack on female rulers, and wrote to Cecil, probably in 1559, to say 'I brought forth Huldah [2 Kings 22, 14] and Deborah; and added, that God did not vainly promise by the mouth of Isaiah, that Queens should be the nursing mothers of the Church.' His letter also supports hereditary right; see *The Works of John Knox*, IV, 357, citing *Zürich Letters*, Second Series, 35.

[133] Knox, *The First Blast of the Trumpet Against the Monstrous Regiment of Women*, 34. Knox tried to wriggle out of his difficulties in the light of Elizabeth's displeasure (and probably Calvin's anger, see above) in a letter to Cecil of 20 July, 1559 but he cannot have made matters better, since he presumed to lecture her there too; see Knox, *Works*, ed. Laing, VI, 47–51.

[134] Knox, *The First Blast of the Trumpet*, 40.

foundation for later theories of shared governance,[135] but it also casts some light on how the reform-minded circle preparing the entry might have thought about biblical exemplars. Aylmer had been tutor to Lady Jane Grey, was the friend of Elizabeth's tutor Roger Ascham, and from 1577 would serve as Elizabeth's bishop of London. Unlike Knox he saw nature as a continuous and therefore reassuring fabric; when God sent a woman to rule over a kingdom where the succession is determined by lineal descent, it was simply an indication of 'some secret purpose ....where was least help of any worldly means, there wrought he greatest wonders and brought things to a most happy end.'[136] Aylmer was hardly devoid of the prejudices of his time about women, but like a good biblical scholar he read typologically, seeing figures living under the New Testament's vision of Christian freedom as the fulfillment of their Old Testament prefigurations. He even cast Anne Boleyn, 'the chief, first and only cause of banishing the beast of Rome, with all his beggarly baggage' in the role of a saving Hester.[137] His point of view was that of the evangelicals surrounding Edward VI, who had so thoroughly excavated the bible for prefigurations of English kingship. Furthermore, in the pageant's verses Deborah was presented not only as consulting her estates, but as a leader in war: 'In war she, through God's aid, did put her foes to flight, / And with the dint of sword the band of bondage brast. / In peace she, through God's aid, did always maintain right / And judged Israel till forty years were passed' (94). Military *virtù* was to be hoped for even in a female monarch.

At the level of practical politics Elizabeth may have been displeased with the Deborah pageant (this is the only one for which her response is not recorded), but its advice would have been cushioned by the implication that she was not only a potentially warlike leader, but also, typologically speaking, a fulfillment of the biblical Queen, just as the comparison of Henry VII with King David had signified the city of York's willingness to come to terms with the new king in 1486.[138] One of the

---

[135] See McLaren, *Political Culture in the Reign of Elizabeth*, especially Chapter 1, '"To be Deborah": the political implications of providentialism under a female ruler' and Hoak, 'A Tudor Deborah?' esp. 74–79.

[136] Aylmer, *An harborowe for faithful and trewe subiects*, B3^r.

[137] Aylmer, *An harborowe for faithful subiectes*, B4^v; for the tale of Hester (Esther), second wife of King Ahasuerus, who saved the Israelites from the destroyer Haman, see Esther 2, esp. 17: 'And the king loved Esther above all the women, and she obtained grace and favour in his sight more than all the virgins; so that he set the royal crown upon her head, and made her queen instead of Vashti.' The allusion is a brilliant illustration of how slippery Tudor allegory could be.

[138] On the treatment of Henry VIII as the fulfilment of the biblical David and Solomon, see MacCulloch, *Tudor Church Militant*, 14; for the parallelling of Edward

deepest-rooted features of previous entries, whether aesthetically accomplished or not, was their stress on the typological relationship between the earthly ruler and his Biblical antecedents. For a reigning queen, however, typological parallels were not so easily available. Elizabeth might see herself as a Daniel, but Daniel merely held offices in Babylon and never ruled Israel; besides, he was a man. Deborah, however, was a feasible typological parallel for the reigning queen of a new Israel, emphasising as almost all previous entries had done the typological connection between the rulers of England and those of Israel. Like her subjects, the Queen read typologically,[139] and she would have noted the way the bitter pill of counsel had been sweetened: 'A worthy precedent, O worthy Queen, thou hast.'

From Ritual into History

The last stages of the entry were at hand. According to Schivenoglia, when Elizabeth passed through Ludgate, where some prisoners of the Mayor of London were held, she pardoned the debtors among them (111), but the pamphlet makes no mention of this example of the mercy that ought to characterize a good ruler.[140] However, shortly after the pageant of Deborah, the Queen passed the children of Christ's Hospital, of which Grafton was Warden, and promised to remember the needs of the poor, which she apparently did with a contribution of ten pounds early in March (126). After some prompting she also acknowledged the money (emphatically stressed in the pamphlet) that the guildsmen had expended to receive her properly. Finally at Temple Bar she encountered the child in poet's garb with his gifts of firm hope and earnest prayer, and was reminded of the popular history of the City by the images of the giants Gotmagot and Corineus, who held up the table explaining the whole entry to her. Then, with the vow 'be ye well assured, I will stand your good Queen,' she processed through the dusk out of the city streets, past frozen gardens and fields towards Westminster.

Elizabeth Tudor had little need of explanatory tables; she was already well instructed in the problems that beset rulers. Seen strictly as a ritual, however, the impact of her royal entry was to turn an untried princess into the woman who could make that firm vow, 'I will stand your good

---

with the boy king Josiah, see Aston, *The King's Bedpost*, 36–37.

[139] For Elizabeth's comparison of herself to Old Testament figures, see prayers 20 and 22 in *The Collected Works of Elizabeth I*, 155 and 157, and the prayer she uttered at the Tower at the beginning of her 1559 entry (98).

[140] Such amnesties may not have been exceptional; the emperor Charles V asked for the freedom of prisoners in the Marshalsea and King's Bench when he entered London in 1522; see Robertson, 'L'entrée de Charles quint à Londres, en 1522,' 174.

Queen.' Prompted by the political agendas of court and council, provided with sumptuous display by guildsmen and artisans, and shaped into a coherent Reformation device by Grafton and Mulcaster, the entry fulfilled the ritual task of incorporating the Queen into the community receiving her, and preparing her for the greater experience of the coronation the next day. With respect to the people of London she was no longer a liminal personage, as yet unready for her task; Mulcaster and Grafton had ensured that she made her promise to them, as God had made his promise to her. With respect to the country as a whole, she had successfully undergone the first part of the ritual experience of becoming its Queen. What her own views were of the experience we can only speculate; Elizabeth loved a good entertainment, though her later actions suggest that she took the unwelcome advice to govern collaboratively with more than a grain of salt. Nevertheless, if the Queen was of a secular mind in politics, she was personally devout, and it would be wrong to think she did not take seriously the preparation she was undergoing.

Yet as is usual in such seemingly traditional events, the everyday intervened; and from their interaction history was made. When the young Queen passed through Temple Bar that Saturday afternoon, it was into the hands of a different group of men, who the next day would conduct her through the religious ceremony of her coronation – courtiers protecting their various offices, nobles watchful over their hereditary functions, the bishop troubled by religious scruples who would reluctantly anoint her. The situation was an uncertain one; the sacred rites would be sustained by customs dating from the time of Edward the Confessor, whose crown the Queen would briefly wear. Yet should the rites of the old religion used for Mary be employed, or the 'old observances and ceremonies...meet for sundry respects to be corrected'[141] that had been devised for the crowning of Edward VI? The Queen's preference for change – conservative change – was known, but her first parliament had yet to meet, the settlement of religion still needed to be engineered, and the conduct of church services, as well as baptisms, weddings and funerals, was only tentatively adapting itself to the new order. Sunday's coronation ceremony at Westminster Abbey, however, foreshadowed what was to come in the next months. The bishops still in place refused to include in the Coronation mass two significantly Protestant elements that were essential to Elizabeth's principles: the host should not be elevated and she should receive communion in both kinds, that is both bread and wine.[142] Nevertheless, Mass according to her preferred form was celebrated by her compliant chaplain, George

---

[141] *Literary Remains of King Edward the Sixth*, I cclxxviii.
[142] Bowers, 'The Chapel Royal, the First Elizabethan Prayer Book, and Elizabeth's Settlement of Religion, 1559,' 327.

Carew, the Queen took communion behind a curtain, and after his fellow-bishops all refused to do so, the coronation oath was reluctantly administered by the Bishop of Carlisle, Owen Oglethorpe. That oath, Dale Hoak argues, was devised by Cecil himself, and included the evangelical phraseology 'according to the Laws of God [and] the true profession of the Gospel established in this kingdom.'[143] With much difficulty, the independent course of the English church had been confirmed.

"A royal virgin shall reign"

Throughout her life, in progresses and public events of all kinds, Elizabeth would make monarchical display a central political device of her rule; in the nineteenth century it took John Nichols three volumes in which to chronicle her progresses. But though earlier English monarchs regularly made a practice of ceremonially 'entering' London (Henry VII, for example, did so several times), we know of very few formal entries Elizabeth made into English towns. In 1571 she entered Saffron Walden and in 1578 Norwich (where the pageants included a reference to Deborah); in 1585 the Pomeranian traveller Lupold von Wedel described another entry into the City. In 1588, after the Armada had been dispersed, she processed to St. Paul's Cathedral, where she humbled herself before the altar and thanked God for saving England.[144]

However, by the time of the old Queen's death in 1603, a major transformation in the symbolic expressiveness of public life had taken place. London was spreading rapidly beyond its medieval walls, and it now had a flourishing tradition of public and private theatre, with playwrights to devise pageants and masques in plenty. Stow's *Survey of London* (1598), observes Stephen Mullaney, records a city that economic, social and cultural changes were making unrecognizable to its own citizens.[145] Furthermore, when the elderly Richard Mulcaster wrote his lament for the Queen's death, he was welcoming at the same time a monarch from distant Scotland, one who knew little of Londoners, and moreover had a personal aversion to public ceremonial. Like other rulers of late Renaissance and baroque states James I was withdrawing into a space from which his subjects were isolated. Though he was crowned in

---

[143] The question of the rites used at Elizabeth's coronation has been much debated; see Haugaard, 'The Coronation of Elizabeth I,' 161–170. Cecil's responsibility for the writing of the oath is argued by Dale Hoak, 'The Coronations of Edward VI, Mary I, and Elizabeth I.'

[144] For Saffron Walden see Nichols, *Progresses* I, 280–281; for Norwich see II, 133–178 and for 1588 (from Somerset House to St. Paul's) see II, 537–542. For von Wedel's diary see von Klarwill, ed., *Queen Elizabeth and Some Foreigners*, 328–329.

[145] Mullaney, *The Place of the Stage*, 15.

July, 1603, his entry was postponed because of the plague, and when it took place in March 1604 he hastened past the elaborate pageants that Thomas Dekker and Ben Jonson had prepared, making no response to them or to the crowds. As Arthur Wilson reported in his 1653 biography, the king 'did not love to be looked upon, and those formalities of state which set a lustre upon Princes in the people's eyes were but so many burthens to him....He was not like his predecessor, the late Queen of famous memory, that with a well-pleased affection met her peoples acclamations, thinking most highly of herself when she was born up on the wings of their humble supplications. He endured this day's brunt with patience, being assured he should never have such another.'[146]

Paradoxically it was the advent of professionals like Dekker and Jonson, with their magnificently crafted spectacles, that helped to widen the breach between the monarch who entered the city and the people who received him. 'The custom of the citizens themselves acting out their identity was no longer observed,' writes Alexandra F. Johnston.[147] 'Representation,' where spectators and participants were distanced from each other in what had become a theatrical occasion, had superseded 'presentation,' where spectators and participants were both involved in the event.[148] James's son Charles I eventually cancelled the entry that the guildsmen had several times attempted to prepare for him.[149] During the Protectorate, the structure of the ruler's court and some of its pomp was maintained, and the City received Cromwell formally in February 1654, in a variation on the traditional ceremony.[150] When Charles II made his royal entry in 1660, marking the restoration of the monarchy, the diarist John Evelyn happily described 'a Triumph of above 20,000 horse and foot, brandishing their swords and shouting with inexpressible joy.' Evelyn himself 'stood in the Strand and beheld it, and blessed God.'[151] But this was the last formal royal entry of an English monarch into the City of London. Considerable effort was made in 1689 to give ceremonial force to the succession of William and Mary,[152] and William III was received by the citizens as late as 16 November 1697.[153] However, as R.O. Bucholz observes, 'In the brave new

---

[146] Wilson, *The History of Great Britain, being The Life and Reign of King James the First*, 12–13.
[147] Johnston, 'English Civic Ceremony,' 400.
[148] Kinser, 'Presentation and Representation," 6.
[149] On Charles I's marked concern with order and decorum and the way it led to his increasing isolation, see Richards, '"His Nowe Majestie"' 70–96.
[150] *Mercurius Politicus*, no. 191, 276. For ceremony surrounding Cromwell, see Sherwood, *The Court of Oliver Cromwell* and Knoppers, *Constructing Cromwell*.
[151] Evelyn, *Diary*, III, 246.
[152] See Schwerer, 'The Glorious Revolution as Spectacle: A New Perspective.'
[153] Withington, *English Pageantry*, I, 252.

political world of postrevolutionary England, ritual, symbol and personal allegiance were coming to mean less and less to an increasingly cosmopolitan, venal, and partisan ruling class.'[154] Though the coronation rite itself today still maintains many of its ancient features,[155] the related customs dictated by the medieval manuals fell into disuse; George II, who succeeded to the crown in 1727, was the last English king to be feasted at a great coronation banquet. However, one feature of the *adventus*/triumph still remains in our repertoire of symbols, the triumphal entry arch representing the city gate, which even today is employed to convey images of territorial glory and civic welcome.

Elizabeth's procession must have been great entertainment for the citizens who watched it, though perhaps a little dignified in comparison with the acrobats and jugglers of other entries. The pageants with their poster-like 'tables' were left standing until the seventeenth of January, so that Londoners could 'wander through the streets and understand the symbolic content of each device.'[156] And the biblical rhetoric of the entry both expressed the evangelical nationalism of its age and foretold the religious conflicts of the century to come. Indeed, the 'voice' (in the literary sense) of the entry pamphlet is in a marked sense that of Reformation England: urgent, almost pedagogic, and deeply committed to the creation of a new monarchical imagery.[157] It also exhibits a profound awareness of the power of its own textuality. 'Elizabeth herself is treated as a text to be read, as an ideal female ruler,' writes Helen Hackett; the Queen 'not only showed herself as a spectacle, but was shown to herself as a spectacle.'[158] The 'unity' central to the pamphlet's message is not implicit and metaphorical, as in Katherine of Aragon's entry, but explicit and discursive, centred firmly in the Protestant idealization of the Word.

There were important long-term consequences of the rapid printing and almost immediate reprinting of the physical pamphlet itself, and its circulation not only among the popular reading public but among the learned who could understand the Latin passages and take up and explore its themes.[159] This was the first printed English 'entry book' to give a full

---

[154]Bucholz, *The Augustan Court*, 250.

[155]For the survival of the coronation *ordo* of 1689, see Schramm, *A History of the English Coronation*, 102–103.

[156]Strong, 'The 1559 Entry Pageants of Elizabeth I,' in his *The Tudor and Stuart Monarchy: Pageantry, Painting Iconography*, 42.

[157]Interestingly it omits a biblical motif prominent in medieval pageants which ought to have attracted Protestant image makers (at it later did Edmund Spenser), that of the City of London as New Jerusalem (Rev. 21); see Kipling, *Enter the King*, 15–17, 345–349.

[158]Hackett, *Virgin Mother, Maiden Queen*, 45, 46.

[159]On the various audiences for the pamphlet see Richards, 'Love and a Female Monarch,' 156–157.

account of an entire procession, including not only the verses but a description of the pageants and the underlying theme of the entire display.[160] The suggestion in the Latin oration presented at St. Paul's Churchyard that the Queen's accession signified the return of the golden age, though rooted in the ancient praises accorded entering monarchs, is also the first hint of a body of imagery that would, in the later years of the Queen's long reign, be deployed to associate her with the goddess Astraea. As we have seen, the comparison to Deborah in the pageant at the conduit in Fleet Street was immediately taken up by the evangelical writer John Aylmer in his *An harborowe for faithfull and trewe subjectes* (1559).

Raphael Holinshed in his *Chronicles of England, Scotlande, and Irelande* (1577, 1587) included the pamphlet's text almost verbatim, and it was also reissued in 1604 at the accession of James I. It was quoted and cited by nostalgic Jacobean authors such as Thomas Heywood. In his play *If You Know Not Me, You Know No Body, or, The Troubles of Queen Elizabeth* (1605) entry and coronation are amalgamated in a miniature version for the stage, and Elizabeth is made to pardon her Tower jailer, one Beningfield. The presentation of the Bible in English is the climax of the scene:

> *Mayor*: I from this City London do present,
> This purse and Bible to your Majesty,
> A thousand of your faithful citizens,
> In velvet coats and chains well mounted, stay
> To greet their royal sovereign on the way.
>
> *Elizabeth*: We thank you all; but first this booke I kiss,
> Thou art the way to honour; thou to bliss,
> An English Bible, thanks my good Lord Mayor,
> You of our body and our soul have care;
> This is the jewel that we still love best,
> This was our solace when we were distressed,
> This book that hath so long concealed itself,
> So long shut up, so long hid; now Lords, see,
> We here unclasp, for ever it is free.[161]

---

[160] Anglo, *Spectacle, Pageantry and Early Tudor Policy*, 189, quotes the translator of the Latin verses for Charles V's 1522 entry into London: 'Why should one write, that each man with his eye / Did well behould and see, wandering to and fro' (modernized). See also Wall, *The Imprint of Gender*, 117–126.

[161] Heywood, *If You Know Not Me, You Know No Body, or, The Troubles of Queen Elizabeth*, ll. 1573–1586. He evidently had recourse to the pamphlet or its recapitulation in Holinshed; his *England's Elizabeth* (1631) gives a lengthy and detailed précis of the events of 1559.

Nostalgia for Elizabeth's reign could cut two ways; 'As seventeenth-century England weathered one constitutional crisis after the next, Elizabeth was more than the object of anti-Stuart nostalgia,' observes John Watkins; 'Her conflicted status as the female head of a patriarchal state became the basis for competing interpretations of the proper relationship between the Crown and people....For Royalists she was always Gloriana, a quasi-divine being from whom power, virtue and legal authority emanated to the realm at large....Parliamentarians, on the other hand, preferred an alternative Elizabeth who yielded to masculine counsel.'[162] After 1688, however, John Strype's recapitulation of Holinshed in his *Annals of the Reformation* (1709) established the pamphlet's image of Elizabeth as the historiographic norm, and its 'narrative of idealized subject-monarch relationships ....was thereby incorporated into the mainstream of English history writing.'[163] The original pamphlet was partly reprinted in 1811 in an edition of Fabyan's *Chronicle*, and fully in John Nichols' three-volume edition of *The Progresses and Public Processions of Queen Elizabeth* (1823). Through such means Mulcaster's spirited account of the Queen's participation in the event, and his polemical framing of the monarchy as dutiful, national and reformed, had an immeasurable influence on the historiography of Elizabeth's reign.

Richard Grafton died about 1572; according to the Minutes of the Grocers' Company, he was receiving company charity at his death, though admittedly his support would have been in proportion to his former status.[164] As for Mulcaster, though he was apparently a difficult man to get along with, he nevertheless flourished as a teacher, a promoter of school drama, and a deviser of pageants. One of Mulcaster's less appealing characteristics was his strong sense (often misguided) of his own entitlement, which led him into quarrels and money troubles throughout his life. But as the dedications of his books show, he was devoted to the Queen, and as a reading of *Positions* and *The Elementarie* suggests, he must have been an enthusiastic, if exacting, teacher of her subjects. Perhaps it was under his tutelage that the young Edmund Spenser – later author of the pageants and processions in *The Faerie Queene* – began to imagine the prophecy of Merlin in FQ III, iii, 49, with its forecast of eternal union between nations, when a royal virgin shall reign, and 'Sacred Peace shall lovingly persuade / The warlike minds, to learne her goodly lore, and civil arms to exercise no more.' The chaste rule of female monarchy had, at least in the England of Elizabeth, triumphed over the military *virtù* of two millennia of European rulers.

---

[162] Watkins, '"Old Bess in the Ruff",' 99, 110.
[163] Richards, 'Love and a Female Monarch,' 158.
[164] Archer, *The Pursuit of Stability*, 122.

The Receiving of the Queen's Majesty

Upon Saturday, which was the fourteenth day of January in the year of our Lord God 1558,[1] about two of the clock in the afternoon, the most noble and Christian princess, our most dread* sovereign Lady Elizabeth, by the grace of God Queen of England, France[2] and Ireland, Defender of the Faith, etc., marched from the Tower to pass through the city of London toward Westminster, richly furnished* and most honourably accompanied as well with gentlemen, barons, and other [of] the nobility of this realm, as also with a notable train of goodly and beautiful ladies richly appointed. And entering the city was of the people received marvellously entirely,[3] as appeared by the assembly, prayers, wishes, welcomings, cries, tender words and all other signs, which argue a wonderful earnest love of most obedient subjects toward their sovereign. And on the other side, her Grace by holding up her hands and merry countenance to such as stood far off, and most tender and gentle language to those that stood nigh to her Grace, did declare herself no less thankfully to receive her people's good will than they lovingly offered it unto her. To all that wished her Grace well, she gave hearty thanks, and to such as bade 'God save her Grace,' she said again 'God save them all,' and thanked them with all her heart. So that on either side there was nothing but gladness, nothing but prayer, nothing but comfort.

The Queen's Majesty rejoiced marvellously to see that so exceedingly showed toward her which all good princes have ever desired, I mean so earnest love of subjects so evidently declared, even to her Grace's own person being carried in the midst of them. The people again were wonderfully ravished with the loving answers and gestures of their princess, like to the which they had before tried* at her first coming to the Tower from Hatfield.*[4] This her Grace's loving behaviour, preconceived in the people's heads upon these considerations, was then

---

[1]In the Tudor period the English began the calendar year on March 25, Lady Day (the feast of the Annunciation).

[2]English title to French territory originated with William the Conqueror and was consolidated by Henry II. In the reign of Mary I the last of that territory, Calais, was lost (1558). The English monarchy's claim to the title itself was not withdrawn until the Treaty of Amiens (1802).

[3]All the people received her very enthusiastically.

[4]At her imprisonment in 1554 (see Introduction).

thoroughly confirmed, and indeed implanted a wonderful hope in them touching her worthy government in the rest of her reign. For in all her passage she did not only show her most gracious love toward the people in general, but also privately.⁵ If the baser* personages had either offered her Grace any flowers or such like as a signification of their good will, or moved to her any suit,⁶ she most gently, to the common rejoicing of all the lookers on, and private comfort of the party, stayed her chariot and heard their requests. So that if a man should say well, he could not better term the city of London at that time than a stage wherein was shown the wonderful spectacle of a noble-hearted princess toward her most loving people, and the people's exceeding comfort in beholding so worthy a sovereign and hearing so princelike a voice which could not but have set the enemy on fire. Since that virtue is in the enemy always commended,⁷ much more could not but inflame her natural, obedient, and most loving people, whose weale* leaneth only upon her Grace and her government.

Thus therefore the Queen's Majesty passed from the Tower till she came to Fenchurch, the people on each side joyously beholding the view of so gracious a Lady their Queen, and her Grace no less gladly noting and observing the same. Near unto Fenchurch was erected a scaffold* richly furnished whereon stood a noise* of instruments and a child in costly apparel, which was appointed to welcome the Queen's Majesty in the whole city's behalf. Against* which place when her Grace came, of her own will she commanded the chariot to be stayed, and that the noise might be appeased⁸ till the child had uttered his welcoming oration, which he spoke in English metre [as] here followeth:

> O peerless sovereign Queen, behold what this thy town
> Hath thee presented with at thy first entrance here:
> Behold with how rich hope she leadeth thee to thy crown
> Behold with what two gifts she comforteth thy cheer.
>
> The first is blessing tongues, which many a welcome say
> Which pray thou mayest do well, which praise thee to the sky
> Which wish to thee long life, which bless this happy day
> Which to thy kingdom heaps, all that in tongues can lie.
>
> The second is true hearts, which love thee from their root
> Whose suit is triumph now, and ruleth all the game.

---

⁵Individually, in person.
⁶Petitioned her or asked for some favour.
⁷That virtue: the power of a prince-like voice.
⁸She asked that the musicians cease playing.

Which faithfulness have won, and all untruth delved out,
Which skip for joy, whenas they hear thy happy name.

Welcome therefore O Queen, as much as heart can think,
Welcome again O Queen, as much as tongue can tell:
Welcome to joyous tongues, and hearts that will not shrink,
God thee preserve we pray, and wish thee ever well.

At which words of the last line the whole people gave a great shout, wishing with one assent as the child had said. And the Queen's Majesty thanked most heartily both the city for this her gentle receiving at the first,[9] and also the people for confirming the same. Here was noted in the Queen's Majesty's countenance, during the time that the child spoke, besides a perpetual attentiveness in her face, a marvellous change in look, as the child's words touched either her person or the people's tongues and hearts. So that she with rejoicing visage did evidently declare that the words took no less place in her mind than they were most heartily pronounced by the child, as from all the hearts of her most hearty citizens. The same verses were fastened up in a table* upon the scaffold, and the Latin thereof, likewise in Latin verses, in another table as hereafter ensueth:

Urbs tua quæ ingressu dederit tibi munera primo,
    O Regina parem non habitura, vide.
Ad diadema tuum, te spe quam divite mittat,
    Quæ duo lætitiæ det tibi dona, vide.
Munus habes primum, linguas bona multa precantes,
    Quæ te quum laudant, tum pia vota sonant,
Fœlicemque diem huuc dicunt, tibi secula longa
    Optant, et quicquid denique lingua potest.
Altera dona feres, vera, et tui amantia corda,
    Quorum gens ludum iam regit una tuum:
In quibus est infracta fides, falsumque perosa,
    Quæque tuo audito nomine læta salit
Grata venis igitur, quantum cor concipit ullum,
    Quantum lingua potest dicere, grata venis.
Cordibus infractis, linguisque per omnia lætis
    Grata venis; salvam te velit esse deus.[10]

Now when the child had pronounced his oration, and the Queen's highness so thankfully had received it, she marched forward towards

---

[9] At the beginning of her reception in the city.

[10] For translations of the Latin passages here and later, see Appendix III; this poem requires no translation, since the text is given first in English, above.

Gracious Street,[11] where at the upper end, before the sign of the Eagle,[12] the city had erected a gorgeous and sumptuous arch, as here followeth:

A stage was made which extended from the one side of the street to the other, richly vaulted with battlements containing three portes*, and over the middlemost was advanced three several* stages in degrees.[13] Upon the lowest stage was made one* seat royal,[14] wherein were placed two personages representing King Henry the seventh and Elizabeth his wife, daughter of King Edward the fourth, either of these two princes sitting under one cloth of estate[15] in their seats, not otherwise divided, but that the one of them which was King Henry the seventh, proceeding out of the house of Lancaster, was enclosed in a red rose, and the other which was Queen Elizabeth, being heir to the house of York, enclosed with a white rose,[16] each of them royally crowned and decently apparelled as apperteineth to princes, with sceptres in their hands, and one vault surmounting their heads, wherein aptly were placed two tables, each containing the title of those two princes. And these personages were so set that the one of them joined hands with the other, with the ring of matrimony perceived on the finger. Out of the which two roses sprang, two branches gathered into one,[17] which were directed upward to the second stage or degree wherein was placed one representing the valiant and noble prince King Henry the eighth, which sprang out of the former stock, crowned with a crown imperial,[18] and by him sat one representing the right worthy Lady Queen Anne, wife to the said King Henry the eighth and mother to our most sovereign Lady Queen Elizabeth that now is, both apparelled with sceptres and diadems and other furniture* due to the estate of a king and queen, and two tables surmounting their heads

---

[11] Gracechurch Street (see map, figure 9)

[12] The tavern in Gracechurch Street known as the Spread Eagle.

[13] Rising upward in a series.

[14] A throne.

[15] A canopy signifying their rank. Judith Richards argues that this signifies they were co-equal monarchs, since the rules ordinarily stipulated separate cloths of estate. See her 'Love and a Female Monarch,' 148.

[16] For the vigorous exploitation of the symbolism of the white and red roses to demonstrate the Tudor title to the throne, see Anglo, *Spectacle, Pageantry and Early Tudor Policy*, 36–37.

[17] Derived from the medieval image of the Tree of Jesse, which illustrated the descent of the kings of Israel, culminating in Christ. For its political exploitation in this period see Hackett, *Virgin Mother, Maiden Queen*, 42.

[18] Not the open circlet of the early medieval English kings, but the crown – first worn by Henry V and still in use today — with two crossed arches rising about it, topped by a cross. The wearer of such a crown is no mere king, but the ruler of a sovereign state as independent as any empire. See Hoak, 'The Iconography of the Crown Imperial,' and Introduction.

wherein were written their names and titles.[19] From their seat also proceeded upwards one branch directed to the third and uppermost stage or degree, wherein likewise was planted a seat royal, in the which was set one representing the Queen's most excellent Majesty Elizabeth now our most dread sovereign Lady, crowned and apparelled as the other princes were. Out of the forepart of this pageant was made a standing* for a child, which at the Queen's Majesty's coming declared unto her the whole meaning of the said pageant. The two sides of the same were filled with loud noises of music. And all empty places thereof were furnished with sentences* concerning unity. And the whole pageant was garnished with red roses and white, and in the forefront of the same pageant in a fair wreath was written the name and title of the same, which was *The Uniting of the Two Houses of Lancaster and York.*

This pageant was grounded* upon the Queen's Majesty's name. For like as the long war between the two houses of York and Lancaster then ended when Elizabeth, daughter to Edward the fourth, matched in marriage with Henry the seventh heir to the house of Lancaster, so since the Queen's Majesty's name is Elizabeth and for so much as she is the only heir of Henry VIII, which came of both the houses as the knitting up of concord, it was devised that like as Elizabeth was the first occasion of concord, so she, another Elizabeth, might maintain the same among her subjects, so that unity was the end whereat the whole device shot,[20] as the Queen's Majesty's name moved the first ground. This pageant now against the Queen's Majesty's coming was addressed with[21] children representing the aforenamed personages, with all furniture due unto the setting forth of such a matter well meant, as the argument declared, costly and sumptuously set forth, as the beholders can bear witness.

Now the Queen's Majesty drew near unto the said pageant, and forsomuch as the noise was great by reason of the press of people, so that she could scarce hear the child which did interpret the said pageant, and her chariot was passed so far forward that she could not well view the personages representing the kings and queens above-named, she required to have the matter opened unto to her,[22] which so was, and every personage appointed, and what they signified, with the end of unity and ground of her name, according as is before expressed. For the sight

---

[19]Schivenoglia (see Appendix I) notes that a pomegranate was set between Henry's two roses; this fruit was a symbol of the Resurrection because of its association with the myth of Persephone, and in the Renaissance it was widely used in the impresas of rulers because its many seeds within a single shell made it a figure of unified authority.
[20]Aimed.
[21]Arranged, prepared with.
[22]Explained to her.

whereof her Grace caused her chariot to be removed back, and yet hardly could she see, because the children were set somewhat with the farthest in.[23] But after that her Grace had understood the meaning thereof, she thanked the city, praised the fairness of the work, and promised that she would do her whole endeavour for the continual preservation of concord, as the pageant did import. The child appointed in the standing above-named to open the meaning of the pageant spoke these words unto her Grace:

> The two princes that sit under one cloth of state,
> The man in the red rose, the woman in the white:
> Henry VII and Queen Elizabeth his mate,
> By ring of marriage as man and wife unite.
>
> Both heirs to both their bloods, to Lancaster the king
> The Queen to York, in one the two houses did knit,
> Of whom as heir to both, Henry the Eighth did spring,
> In whose seat his true heir thou Queen Elizabeth now sit.
>
> Therefore as civil war, and shed of blood did cease,
> When these two houses were united into one
> So now that jar* shall stint, and quietness increase,
> We trust, O noble Queen, thou will be cause alone.

The which also were written in Latin verses, and both drawn in two tables upon the forefront of the said pageant as hereafter followeth:

> *Hii quos iungit idem solium quos annulus idem*
> *Hæc albente nitens, ille rubente Rosa:*
> *Septimus Henricus Rex, Regina Elizabetha,*
> *Scilicet Hæredes gentis uterque suæ:*
> *Hæc Eboracensis, Lancastrius ille dederunt*
> *Connubio, e geminis quo foret una domus*
> *Excipit hos hæres Henricus copula regum*
> *Octavus, magni Regis imago potens*
> *Regibus hinc succedis avis, Regique parenti*
> *Patris iusta hæres Elizabetha tui.*[24]

¶ Sentences placed therein concerning unity.

Nullæ concordes animos vires domant.
Qui iuncti terrent, deiuncti timent.
Discordes animi solvunt, concordes ligant.

---

[23] Some of the children were too close to the front of the pageant.
[24] The Latin poem repeats the English one, but without the last four lines referring to the Wars of the Roses.

Augentur parva pace, magna bello cadunt.
Coniunctæ manus fortius tollunt onus.
Regno pro menibus æneis civium concordia.
Que diu pugnant diutius lugent.
Dissidentes principes sulditorum lues.
Princeps ad pacem natus non ad arma datur
Filia concordiæ copia, neptis quies.
Dissentiens respublica hostibus placet.
Qui idem tenent, diutius tenent.
Regnum divisum facile dissolvitur.
Civitas concors armis frustra tentatur.
Omnium gentium consensus firmat fidem. &c

These verses and other pretty* sentences were drawn in void* places of this pageant, all tending to one end, that quietness might be maintained and all dissension displaced, and that by the Queen's Majesty, heir to agreement, and agreeing in name with her which tofore* had joined those houses, which had been the occasion of much debate and civil war within this realm; as may appear to such as will search chronicles,[25] but be not to be touched in this treatise, only declaring her Grace's passage through the city, and what provision the city made therefor. And ere the Queen's Majesty came within hearing of this pageant, she sent certain [persons] as also at all the other pageants, to require the people to be silent, for her Majesty was disposed to hear all that should be said unto her.

When the Queen's Majesty had heard the child's oration and understood the meaning of the pageant at large, she marched forward toward Cornhill, always received with like rejoicing of the people, and there as her Grace passed by the conduit which was curiously trimmed against that time[26] with rich banners adorned, and a noise of loud instruments upon the top thereof, she espied the second pageant, and because she feared for the people's noise that she should not hear the child which did expound the same, she enquired what that pageant was ere that she came to it. And there understood that there was a child representing her Majesty's person, placed in a seat of government, supported by certain virtues which suppressed their contrary vices under their feet, and so forth as in the description of the said pageant shall hereafter appear.

This pageant standing in the nether* end of Cornhill was extended from the one side of the street to the other, and in the same pageant was devised three gates all open and over the middle part thereof was erected one chair, a seat royal with cloth of estate to the same appertaining, wherein was placed a child representing the Queen's highness, with

---

[25]To those who look through the old chronicles of English history.
[26]Arfully decorated for the occasion.

consideration had for [a] place convenient for a table which contained her name and title, and in a comely wreath artificially* and well devised with perfect sight and understanding to the people. In the front of the same pageant was written the name and title thereof, which is *The seat of worthy governance*, which seat was made in such artificial manner as to the appearance of the lookers on the forepart seemed to have no stay, and therefore of force was stayed by lively personages[27], which personages were in number four, standing and staying the forefront of the same seat royal, each having his face to the Queen and people, whereof every one had a table to express their effects[28] which are virtues, namely *Pure religion, Love of subjects, Wisdom,* and *Justice,* which did tread their contrary vices under their feet. That is to wit, *Pure religion* did tread upon *Superstition* and *Ignorance*; *Love of subjects* did tread upon *Rebellion* and *Insolence*; *Wisdom* did tread upon *Folly* and *Vainglory*; *Justice* did tread upon *Adulation* and *Bribery*. Each of these personages, according to their proper* names and properties, had not only their names in plain and perfect writing set upon their breasts easily to be read of all, but also every one of them was aptly and properly apparelled, so that his apparel and name did agree to express the same person that in title he represented. This part of the pageant was thus appointed and furnished. The two sides over the two side portes had in them placed a noise of instruments, which immediately after the child's speech gave [out] a heavenly melody. Upon the top or uppermost part of the said pageant stood the arms of England royally portrayed with the proper beasts to uphold the same.[29] One representing the Queen's highness sat in this seat crowned with an imperial crown, and before her seat was a convenient place appointed for one child, which did interpret and apply the said pageant as hereafter shall be declared. Every void place was furnished with proper sentences commending the seat supported by virtues, and defaming the vices, to the utter extirpation of rebellion and to everlasting continuance of quietness and peace.

The Queen's Majesty approaching nigh unto this pageant thus beautified and furnished in all points, caused her chariot to be drawn nigh thereunto, that her Grace might hear the child's oration, which was this.

> While that religion true, shall ignorance suppress
> And with her weighty foot break superstition's head
> While love of subjects shall rebellion distress
> And with zeal to the prince, insolence downtread.

---

[27]It appeared to the lookers-on that the forepart had no support, and was actually held up by human beings.
[28]Meaning, significance.
[29]In the Tudor period these would have been the lion and the red dragon.

While justice can flattering tongues and bribery deface
While folly and vainglory to wisdom yield their hands
So long shall government not swerve from her right race
But wrong decayeth still, and rightwiseness up stands.

Now all thy subjects' hearts, O prince of peerless fame
Do trust these virtues shall maintain up thy throne,
And vice be kept down still, the wicked put to shame
That good with good may joy, and naught with naught may moan.

Which verses were painted upon the right side of the same pageant, and the Latin thereof[30] on the left side in another table, which were these.

Quæ subnixa alte solio regina superbo est,
    Effigies sanctæ principis alma refert,
Quam civilis amor fulcit, sapientia firmat,
    Iusticia illustrat, Relligioque beat.
Vana superstitio et crassæ ignorantia frontis
    Pressæ sub pura relligine iacent.
Regis amor domat effrenes, animosque rebelles
    Iustus adulantes, Domiuorosque terit.
Cum regit imperium sapiens, sine luce sedebunt
    Stulticia, atque huius numen inanis honor.

Beside these verses there were placed in every void room of the pageant, both in English and Latin, such sentences as advanced the seat of governance upheld by virtue.[31] The ground of this pageant was that like as by virtues (which do abundantly appear in her Grace) the Queen's Majesty was established in the seat of government, so she should sit fast in the same so long as she embraced virtue and held vice underfoot. For if vice once got up the head, it would put the seat of government in peril of falling. The Queen's Majesty when she had heard the child and understood the pageant at full, gave the city also thanks there, and most graciously promised her good endeavour for the maintenance of the said virtues and suppression of vices, and so marched on till she came against the Great Conduit* in Cheap*, which was beautified with pictures and sentences accordingly against her Grace's coming thither.

Against Soper Lane's end was extended from the one side of the street to the other a pageant which had three gates, all open. Over the middlemost whereof were erected three several stages, whereon sat eight children as hereafter followeth. On the uppermost one child, on the

---

[30]The Latin and English verses are somewhat different, as comparison shows. 'Folly' in line 9 is the traditional feminine personification Stultitia, thus '*her* godhead' in line 10.

[31]Argued that virtue should uphold government.

middle three, on the lowest four, each having the proper name of the blessing that they did represent written in a table and placed above their heads. In the forefront of this pageant, before the children which did represent the blessings, was a convenient standing cast out for a child to stand, which did expound the said pageant unto the Queen's Majesty, as was done in the others tofore. Every one of these children were appointed and apparelled according unto the blessing which he did represent. And on the forepart of the said pageant was written in fair letters the name of the said pageant in this manner following:

> *The eight beatitudes expressed in the*
> *fifth chapter of the gospel of St Matthew, applied to our*
> *sovereign lady Queen Elizabeth.*

Over the two side portes was placed a noise of instruments. And all void places in the pageant were furnished with pretty sayings commending and touching the meaning of the said pageant, which was the promises and blessings of Almighty God made to his people. Before that the Queen's highness came unto this pageant, she required the matter somewhat to be opened[32] unto her, that her Grace might better understand what should afterward by the child be said unto her. Which so was, that the city had there erected the pageant with eight children representing the eight blessings touched [upon] in the fifth chapter of St Matthew, whereof every one upon just considerations was applied to her highness. And that the people thereby put her Grace in mind that as her good doings before had given just occasion why that these blessings might fall upon her, that so if her Grace did continue in her goodness as she had entered[33] she should hope for the fruit of these promises due unto them that do exercise themselves in the blessings. Which her Grace heard marvellously graciously, and required that the chariot might be removed towards the pageant that she might perceive the child's words, which were these, the Queen's Majesty giving most attentive ear and requiring that the people's noise might be stayed.

> Thou hast been eight times blessed, O Queen of worthy fame
> By meekness of thy spirit, when care did thee beset
> By mourning in thy grief, by mildness in thy blame[34]
> By hunger and by thirst, and justice couldst none get.

---

[32] Asked for some explanation.
[33] As she had begun.
[34] By acting mildly towards those who had wronged her.

> By mercy shown, not felt, by cleanness of thine heart
> By seeking peace always, by persecution wrong,
> Therefore trust thou in God, since He hath helped thy smart
> That as His promise is, so He will make thee strong.

When these words were spoken, all the people wished that as the child had spoken, so God would strengthen her Grace against all her adversaries, whom the Queen's Majesty did most gently thank for their loving wish. These verses were painted on the left side of the said pageant, and others in Latin on the other side, which were these:

> *Qui lugent hilares fient, qui mitia gestant*
> *Pectora, multa soli iugera culta metent*
> *Iustitiam esuriens sitiensue replebitur, ipsum.*
> *Fas homini puro corde videre deum*
> *Quem alterius miseret dominus miserebitur huius,*
> *Pacificus quisquis, filius ille Dei est.*
> *Propter iustitiam quisquis patietur habetque*
> *Demissam mentem, cælica regna capit.*
> *Huic hominum generi terram, mare, sidera vovit*
> *Omnipotens, horum quisque beatus erit.*

Besides these, every void place in the pageant was furnished with sentences touching the matter and ground of the said pageant. When all that was to be said in this pageant was ended, the Queen's Majesty passed on forward in Cheapside.

At the Standard* in Cheap, which was dressed fair against the time,[35] was placed a noise of trumpets with banners and other furniture. The Cross[36] likewise was also made fair and well trimmed. And near unto the same, upon the porch of Saint Peter's church door, stood the waits of the city,[37] which did give a pleasant noise with their instruments as the Queen's Majesty did pass by, which on every side cast her countenance[38] and wished well to all her most loving people. Soon after that her Grace passed the cross, she had espied the pageant erected at the Little Conduit in Cheap, and incontinent* required to know what it might signify. And it was told her Grace, that there was placed Time. 'Time,' quoth she, 'and Time hath brought me hither.' And so forth the whole matter was opened to her Grace as hereafter shall be declared in the description of the

---

[35] Decorated beautifully for the occasion.

[36] One of the twelve crosses erected in 1290 by Edward I to commemorate the nightly pauses in the funeral procession of his queen, Eleanor of Castile, as it travelled towards London. See Introduction, and figure 11.

[37] A small band playing wind instruments, financially maintained by the city.

[38] Who looked about her on every side.

pageant. But in the opening, when her Grace understood that the Bible in English should be delivered unto her by Truth, which was therein represented by a child, she thanked the city for that gift and said that she would oftentimes read over that book, commanding Sir John Parrat,[39] one of the knights which held up her canopy, to go before and to receive the book. But learning that it should be delivered unto her Grace down by a silken lace, she caused him to stay, and so passed forward till she came against the aldermen in the high end of Cheap tofore the Little Conduit,[40] where the companies of the city ended, which began at Fenchurch and stood along the streets one by another, enclosed with rails hanged with cloths, and themselves well apparelled with many rich furs and their livery hoods[41] upon their shoulders in comely and seemly manner, having before them sundry persons well apparelled in silks and chains of gold, [such] as wifflers* and guarders of the said companies, beside a number of rich hangings as well of tapestry, arras,[42] cloths of gold, silver, velvet, damask, satin, and other silks plentifully hung all the way as the Queen's highness passed from the Tower through the city. Out at the windows and penthouses* of every house did hang a number of rich and costly banners and streamers, till her Grace came to the upper end of Cheap.

And there by appointment, the right worshipful master Ranulph Cholmley, Recorder of the City,[43] presented to the Queen's Majesty a purse of crimson satin richly wrought with gold, wherein the City gave unto the Queen's Majesty a thousand marks in gold, as master Recorder did declare briefly unto the Queen's Majesty, whose words tended to this end: that the Lord Mayor, his brethren, and the commonalty of the City, to declare their gladness and good will towards the Queen's Majesty did present her Grace with that gold, desiring her Grace to continue their good and gracious Queen, and not to esteem the value of the gift but the mind of the givers. The Queen's Majesty with both her hands took the purse, and answered to him, again marvellously pithily, and so pithily that the standers by, as they embraced entirely her gracious answer, so they marvelled at the couching thereof, which was in words truly reported these: 'I thank my lord mayor, his brethren, and you all. And whereas your request is that I should continue your good lady and Queen, be ye

---

[39] For Sir John Parrat [or Perrot] see Introduction.

[40] The westernmost end of Cheapside, at the Little Conduit in front of the church of St. Michael le Querne (see figure 13).

[41] Each London company had a distinctive garb or livery; see also the description by Schivenoglia (Appendix I).

[42] Tapestry hangings with woven scenes and pictures, typically made in Arras, France.

[43] Then, as now, the Recorder is the chief legal officer of the City of London, taking precedence in the Court of Aldermen over all who have not served as Lord Mayor.

ensured that I will be as good unto you as ever Queen was to her people. No will in me can lack, neither do I trust shall there lack any power. And persuade yourselves that for the safety and quietness of you all, I will not spare, if need be, to spend my blood. God thank you all.' Which answer of so noble an hearted princess[44] if it moved a marvellous shout and rejoicing, it is nothing to be marvelled at, since both the heartiness thereof was so wonderful, and the words so jointly knit.[45]

When her Grace had thus answered the Recorder, she marched toward the Little Conduit, where was erected a pageant with square proportion,[46] standing directly before the same conduit, with battlements accordingly. And in the same pageant was advanced two hills or mountains of convenient height. The one of them being on the north side of the same pageant was made cragged, barren and stony, in the which was erected one tree artificially made, all withered and dead, with branches accordingly. And under the same tree, at the foot thereof, sat one in homely and rude apparel, crookedly and in mourning manner, having over his head in a table written in Latin and English, his name, which was *Ruinosa Respublica*, A Decayed Commonweal. And upon the same withered tree were fixed certain tables, wherein were written proper sentences expressing the causes of the decay of a commonweal. The other hill on the south side was made fair, fresh, green and beautiful, the ground thereof full of flowers and beauty, and on the same was erected also one tree very fresh and fair, under the which stood upright one fresh personage well apparelled and appointed, whose name also was written both in English and in Latin, which was *Respublica bene instituta*, A Flourishing Commonweal. And upon the same tree also were fixed certain tables containing sentences which expressed the causes of a flourishing commonweal. In the middle between the said hills was made artificially one hollow place or cave, with [a] door and lock enclosed, out of the which, a little before the Queen's highness's coming thither, issued one personage whose name was *Time*, apparelled as an old man with a scythe in his hand, having wings artificially made, leading a personage of lesser stature than himself, which was finely and well apparelled, all clad in white silk, and directly over her head was set her name and title in Latin and English, *Temporis filia*, the Daughter of Time.[47] Which two so appointed went forward toward the south side of the pageant. And on her breast was written her proper name, which was *Veritas*, Truth, who held a book in her hand upon the which was written *Verbum veritatis*,

---

[44] So noble-hearted
[45] Were rhetorically so well organized.
[46] That is, a square structure, not an arch.
[47] For the history and significance of this important motif, see Introduction.

the Word of Truth. And out of the south side of the pageant was cast a standing for a child which should interpret the same pageant. Against whom, when the Queen's Majesty came, he spoke unto her Grace these words.

> This old man with the scythe, old Father Time they call,
> And her his daughter Truth, which holdeth yonder book
> Whom he out of this rock hath brought forth to us all
> From whence this many years she durst not once out look.
>
> The ruthful wight[48] that sitteth under the barren tree,
> Resembleth to us the form, when commonweals decay
> But when they be in state triumphant, you may see
> By him in fresh attire that sitteth under the bay.[49]
>
> Now since that Time again his daughter Truth hath brought
> We trust O worthy Queen, thou wilt this truth embrace.
> And since thou understandst the good estate and nought
> We trust wealth thou wilt plant, and barrenness displace.
>
> But for to heal the sore, and cure that is not seen,
> Which thing the book of truth doth teach in writing plain:
> She doth present to thee the same, O worthy Queen,
> For that, that words do fly, but writing doth remain.

When the child had thus ended his speech, he reached his book towards the Queen's Majesty, which a little before Truth had let down unto him from the hill, which by master Parrat was received and delivered unto the Queen. But she, as soon as she had received the book, kissed it and with both hands held up the same, and so laid it upon her breast, with great thanks to the city therefor, and so went forward towards Paul's churchyard. The former matter which was rehearsed unto the Queen's Majesty was written in two tables, on either side [of] the pageant eight verses, and in the middest there in Latin:

> *Ille, vides falcem læva qui sustinet uncam,*[50]
> *Tempus is est, cui stat filia vera comes*
> *Hanc pater exesa deductam rupe reponit*
> *In lucem, quam non viderat ante diu*
> *Qui sedet a læva cultu male tristis inepto*
> *Quem duris crescens cautibus orbis obit*
> *Nos monet effigie, qua sit respublica quando*

---

[48]Pitiable creature.

[49]The other tree, which was a bay or laurel, the traditional symbol of glory or renown.

[50]The Latin verses render only the first two stanzas of the English poem.

Corruit, at contra quando beata viget.
Ille docet iuvenis forma spectandus amictu
Scitus, et æterna laurea fronde virens.

The sentences written in Latin and English upon both the trees, declaring the causes of both estates, were these:

¶Causes of a ruinous commonweal are these:

Want of the fear of God.	*Blindness of guides.*
Disobedience to rulers.	*Bribery in magistrates.*
Rebellion in subjects.	*Unmercifulness in rulers.*
Civil disagreement.	*Unthankfulness in subjects.*
Flattering of princes.	

¶Causes of a flourishing commonweal:

Fear of God.	*Obedient subjects.*
A wise prince.	*Lovers of the common weal.*
Learned rulers.	*Virtue rewarded.*
Obedience to officers.	*Vice chastened.*

The matter of this pageant dependeth of them that went before. For as the first declared her Grace to come out[51] of the house of unity, the second showed that she is placed in the seat of government stayed with virtues to the suppression of vice, and therefore in the third the eight blessings of Almighty God might well be applied unto her. So this fourth now is to put her Grace in remembrance of the state of the commonweal which Time with Truth his daughter doth reveal, which Truth also her Grace hath received, and therefore cannot but be merciful and careful for the good government thereof. From thence the Queen's Majesty passed toward Paul's churchyard. And when she came over against Paul's school, a child appointed by the schoolmaster thereof pronounced a certain oration in Latin and certain verses, which were also there written, as followeth.

Philosophus ille divinus Plato inter multa preclare ac sapienter dicta, hoc posteris proditum reliquit, Rempublicam illam fœlicisimam fore, cui princeps sophiæ studiosa, virtutibusque ornata contigerit.[52] Quem si vere dixisse censeamus (ut quidem verissime) cur non terra Britannica plauderet? cur non populus gaudium atque lætitiam agitaret? immo, cur non hunc diem

---

[51]That she was descended from.
[52]'That republic shall be happiest whose prince is learned in wisdom and adorned with virtues,' Plato, *Republic* vii.

albo (quod aiunt) lapillo notaret?[53] *quo princeps talis nobis adest, qualem priores non viderunt, qualemque posteritas haud facile cernere poterit, dotibus quum animi, tum corporis undique fœlicissima. Casti quidem corporis dotes ita apertæ sunt, ut oratione non egeant. Animi vero tot tantæque, ut ne verbis quidem exprimi possint. Haec nempe Regibus summis orta, morum atque animi nobilitate genus exuperat. Huius pectus Cristi religionis amore flagrat. Hæc gentem Britannicam virtutibus illustrabit, clipeoque iustitiæ teget. Haec literis graecis et latinis eximia, ingenioque prepollens est. Hac imperante pietas vigebit, Anglia florebit, aurea secula redibunt. Vos igitur Angli tot commoda accepturi Elizabetham Reginam nostram celeberrimam ab ipso Christo huius regni imperio destinatam, honore debito prosequimini. Huius imperiis animo libentissimo subditi estote, vosque tali principe dignos prebete. Et quoniam pueri non viribus sed precibus officium prestare possunt, nos Alumni huius scholæ ab ipso Coleto olim Templi Paulini Decano,*[54] *extructæ, teneras palmas ad cœlum tendentes Christum Optimum Maximum precaturi sumus ut tuam celsitudinem annos Nestoreos*[55] *summo cum honore Anglis imperitare faciat, matremque pignoribus charis*[56] *beatam reddat. Amen.*

> *Anglia nunc tandem plaudas, lætare, resulta,*
> *Presto iam vita est, præsidiumque tibi*
> *En tua spes venit tua gloria, lux, decus omne*
> *Venit iam solidam quæ tibi prestat opem.*
> *Succurretque tuis rebus quæ pessum abiere.*
> *Perdita quæ fuerant hæc reparare volet*
> *Omnia florebunt, redeunt nunc aurea secla.*
> *In melius surgent quæ cecidere bona.*
> *Debes ergo illi totam te reddere fidam*
> *Cuius in accessu commoda tot capies.*
> *Salue igitur dicas, imo de pectore summo.*
> *Elizabeth Regni non dubitanda salus,*
> *Virgo venit, veniatque optes comitata deinceps.*
> *Pignoribus charis, læta parens veniat*
> *Hoc deus omnipotens ex alto donet olympo*
> *Qui cœlum & terram condidit atque regit.*

Which the Queen's Majesty most attentively harkened unto. And when the child had pronounced [it], he did kiss the oration which he had there

---

[53] In Roman times, a day 'marked with a white stone' was happy; one marked with black was inauspicious.

[54] The Tudor humanist and teacher John Colet (1467–1519), Dean of St. Paul's Cathedral and founder of St. Paul's School.

[55] Nestor, King of Pylos, sailed with the Argonauts and fought at Troy; he was the archetype of wisdom and long life.

[56] 'Dearest pledges,' a poetic commonplace for children.

fair written in paper, and delivered it unto the Queen's Majesty, which most gently received the same.

And when the Queen's Majesty had heard all that was there offered to be spoken, then her Grace marched toward Ludgate where she was received with a noise of instruments, the fore-front of the gate being finely trimmed up against her Majesty's coming.[57] From thence by the way as she went down toward Fleet bridge, one about[58] her Grace noted the City's charge*, that there was no cost spared. Her Grace answered that she did well consider the same, and that it should be remembered. An honourable answer worthy a noble prince, which may comfort all her subjects, considering there can be no point of gentleness or obedient love showed toward her Grace, which she doth not most tenderly accept and graciously weigh. In this manner, the people on either side rejoicing, her Grace went forward toward the conduit in Fleet Street, where was the fifth and last pageant, erected in form following.

From the conduit which was beautified with painting, unto the north side of the street, was erected a stage embattled with four towers, and in the same a square plat rising with degrees,[59] and upon the uppermost degree was placed a chair or seat royal, and behind the same seat, in curious, artificial manner was erected a tree of reasonable height and so far advanced above the seat as it did well and seemly shadow the same without endamaging the sight of any part of the pageant, and the same tree was beautified with leaves as green as art could devise, being of a convenient greatness and containing thereupon the fruit of the date, and on the top of the same tree in a table was set the name thereof which was *A Palm tree*, and in the aforesaid seat or chair was placed a seemly and meet personage richly apparelled in parliament robes, with a sceptre in her hand, as a Queen, crowned with an open crown, whose name and title was in a table fixed over her head in this sort: *Deborah the judge and restorer of the house of Israel. Judges 4.* And the other degrees on either side were furnished with six personages, two representing the nobility, two the clergy, and two the commonalty. And before these personages was written in a table *Deborah with her estates, consulting for the good government of Israel.*[60] At the feet of these and the lowest part of the pageant was ordained a convenient room for a child to open the meaning

---

[57]Ludgate contained a prison for minor criminals. Schivenoglia reports that at this point in the procession Elizabeth freed a number of debtors (see Appendix I); oddly, the pamphlet makes no mention of this demonstration of princely mercy.

[58]Waiting on; or possibly nearby.

[59]A square platform with several levels.

[60]For the critical significance of this pageant, and a possible reason for Deborah's open (as opposed to imperial) crown, see Introduction. For Deborah, see Judges 4 and 5.

of the pageant. When the Queen's Majesty drew near unto this pageant and perceived, as in the other, the child ready to speak, her Grace required silence and commanded her chariot to be removed nigher that she might plainly hear the child speak, which said as hereafter followeth:

> Jaben of Canaan king had long by force of arms
> Oppressed the Israelites, which for God's people went[61]
> But God minding at last for to redress their harms,
> The worthy Deborah as judge among them sent.
>
> In war she, through God's aid, did put her foes to flight,
> And with the dint of sword the band of bondage brast.[62]
> In peace she, through God's aid, did always maintain right
> And judged Israel till forty years were passed.[63]
>
> A worthy precedent, O worthy Queen, thou hast,
> A worthy woman judge, a woman sent for stay,
> And that the like to us endure always thou mayest
> Thy loving subjects will with true hearts and tongues pray.

Which verses were written upon the pageant, and the same in Latin also.

> *Quando dei populum Canaan, rex pressit Iaben,*
> *Mittitur a magno Debora magna deo:*
> *Quæ populum eriperet, sanctum seruaret Iudan,*
> *Milite quæ patrio frangeret hostis opes.*
> *Hæc domino mandante deo lectissima fecit*
> *Fœmina, et aduersos contudit ense viros*
> *Hæc quater denos populum correxerat annos*
> *Iudicio, bello strenua, pace grauis.*
> *Sic, O sic populum belloque et pace guberna,*
> *Debora sis Anglis Elizabetha tuis.*

The void places of the pageant were filled with pretty sentences concerning the same matter. The ground of this last pageant was, that forasmuch as the next pageant before had set before her Grace's eyes the flourishing and desolate states of a commonweal, she might by this be put in remembrance to consult for the worthy government of her people, considering God oftimes sent women nobly to rule among men, as Deborah which governed Israel in peace the space of forty years, and

---

[61]Who were known as God's people. For Jaben, see Judges 4: 2,3.

[62]Burst ('brast,' rhyming with passed).

[63]The bible says nothing about the length of time Deborah judged Israel; it was Deborah's general Barak who reigned for forty years. Grafton is more precise in the 1570 version of his *Chronicle*; he says Deborah reigned for eleven years (see Appendix I).

that it behooves both men and women, so ruling, to use advice of good counsel.

When the Queen's Majesty had passed this pageant, she marched toward Temple Bar. But at St. Dunstan's church, where the children of the Hospital[64] were appointed to stand with their governors, her Grace, perceiving a child offered to make an oration unto her, stayed her chariot and did cast up her eyes to Heaven, as who should say 'I here see this merciful work toward the poor, whom I must in the midst of my royalty needs remember,' and so turned her face toward the child, which in Latin pronounced an oration to this effect: that after the Queen's highness had passed through the City and had seen so sumptuous, rich, and notable spectacles of the citizens, which declared their most hearty receiving and joyous welcoming of her Grace into the same, this one spectacle yet rested and remained, which was the everlasting spectacle of mercy unto the poor members of almighty God, furthered by that famous and most noble prince King Henry the Eighth, her Grace's father, erected by the City of London, and advanced by the most godly, virtuous and gracious prince King Edward VI, her Grace's dear and loving brother,[65] doubting nothing of the mercy of the Queen's most gracious clemency by the which they may not only be relieved and helped, but also stayed and defended, and therefore incessantly they would pray and cry unto Almighty God for the long life and reign of her highness with most prosperous victory against her enemies.

The child after he had ended his oration, kissed the paper wherein the same was written and reached it to the Queen's Majesty, which received it graciously both with words and countenance, declaring her gracious mind toward their relief.[66] From thence her Grace came to Temple Bar, which was dressed finely with the two images of Gotmagot the Albion, and Corineus the Briton,[67] two giants big in stature furnished accordingly,

---

[64]The children of Christ's Hospital, a school for poor children founded on the site of the Greyfriars, the former Franciscan monastery in Newgate Street. Richard Grafton, who held property and lived in Greyfriars, had been Treasurer-General of the Royal Hospitals in 1553–1555, and was closely involved with Christ's Hospital (Kingdon, *Richard Grafton, Citizen and Grocer of London*, 78, 89). He may have been one of the 'governors' standing with the children. For today's 'Blue Coat' students, see figure 5b. St. Dunstan's in the West is in Fleet Street.

[65]Henry VIII dissolved the monasteries, including that of the Greyfriars, between 1536 and 1540; Edward VI used their precincts to establish London's Royal Hospitals shortly before his death in 1553.

[66]It appears she remembered her promise; on 4 March, 1559 her sub-almoner brought the aldermen ten pounds for the relief of the City's poor; see Appendix II.

[67]For Gotmagot and Corineus see Introduction and, as Gog and Magog, figure 5a.

which held in their hands even above the gate a table wherein was written in Latin verses the effect of all the pageants which the City before had erected, which verses were these,

> *Ecce sub aspectu iam contemplaberis uno*
> *O princeps populi sola columna tui.*
> *Quicquid in immensa passim perspexeris urbe*
> *Quæ cepere omnes unus hic arcus habet.*
> *Primus te solio regni donauit auiti,*
> *Hæres quippe tui vera parentis eras.*
> *Suppressis vitiis, domina virtute, Secundus*
> *Firmauit sedem regia virgo tuam.*
> *Tertius ex omni posuit te parte beatam*
> *Si, qua cœpisti pergere velle, velis.*
> *Quarto quid verum, respublica lapsa quid esset*
> *Quæ florens staret te docuere tui.*
> *Quinto magna loco monuit te Debora, missam*
> *Cœlitus in regni gaudia longa tui.*
> *Perge ergo regina, tuæ spes unica gentis,*
> *Hæc postrema urbis suscipe vota tuæ.*
> *Vive diu, regnaque diu, virtutibus orna*
> *Rem patriam, et populi spem tueare tui.*
> *Sic o sic petitur cœlum Sic itur in astra*
> *Hoc virtutis opus, cætera mortis erunt.*

Which verses were also written in English metre in a less[er] table as hereafter followeth:

> Behold here in one view, thou mayest see all that plain
> O princess to this thy people the only stay:
> What elsewhere thou hast seen in this wide town, again
> This one arch, whatsoever the rest contained, doth say.
>
> The first arch as true heir unto thy father dear,
> Did set thee in the throne where thy grandfather sat,
> The second did confirm thy seat as princess here,
> Virtues now bearing sway, and vices beat down flat.
>
> The third, if that thou wouldst go on as thou began,
> Declared thee to be blessed on every side,
> The fourth did open Truth, and also taught thee when
> The commonweal stood well, and when it did thence slide.
>
> The fifth as Deborah declared thee to be sent
> From Heaven, a long comfort to us thy subjects all,
> Therefore go on O Queen, on whom our hope [is] so bent,
> And take with thee this wish of thy town as final,

> Live long, and as long reign, adorning thy country,
> With virtues, and maintain thy people's hope of thee,
> For thus, thus Heaven is won, thus must ye pierce the sky,
> This is by virtue wrought, all other must needs die.

On the south side was appointed by the City a noise of singing children, and one child richly attired as a poet,[68] which gave the Queen's Majesty her farewell in the name of the whole City, by these words:

> As at thine entrance first, O prince of high renown,
> Thou wast presented with tongues & hearts for thy fare,
> So now since thou must needs depart out of this town
> This city sendeth thee firm hope and earnest prayer,
>
> For all men hope in thee, that all virtues shall reign,
> For all men hope that thou, none error wilt support,
> For all men hope that thou wilt truth restore again,
> And mend that is amiss, to all good mens comfort.
>
> And for this hope they pray, thou mayest continue long,
> Our Queen amongst us here, all vice for to supplant,
> And for this hope they pray that God may make thee strong
> As by his grace puissant, so in his truth constant.
>
> Farewell O worthy Queen, and as our hope is sure,
> That into error's place, thou wilt now truth restore,
> So trust we that thou wilt our sovereign Queen endure,
> And loving Lady stand, from henceforth evermore.

While these words were in saying, and certain wishes therein repeated for maintenance of truth and rooting out of error, she now and then held up her hands to heavenward and willed the people to say Amen.

When the child had ended, she said 'be ye well assured, I will stand your good Queen.' At which saying her Grace departed forth through Temple Bar toward Westminster with no less shooting and crying of the people, than she entered the City with a noise of ordinance which the Tower shot off at her Grace's entrance first into Tower street.

The child's saying was also in Latin verses written in a table which was hanged up there:

> *O Regina potens, quum primam urbem ingredereris*
> *Dona tibi, linguas fidaque corda dedit*
> *Discedenti etiam tibi nunc duo munera mittit.*
> *Omina plena spei, votaque plena precum.*

---

[68]It is uncertain what this garb might have been; a toga is possible, given the eclecticism of Tudor constuming.

*Quippe tuis spes est, in te quod provida virtus
    Rexerit, errori nec locus ullus erit.
Quippe tuis spes est, quod tu verum omne reduces
    Solatura bonas, dum mala tollis, opes.
Hac spe freti orant, longum ut Regina gubernes,
    Et regni excindas crimina cuncta tui.
Hac spe freti orant, divina ut gratia fortem,
    Et veræ fidei te velit esse basin.
Iam Regina vale, et sicut nos spes tenet una,
    Quod vero inducto, perditus error erit.
Sic quoque speramus quod eris Regina benigna
    Nobis per regni tempora longa tui.*

Thus the Queen's highness passed through the City, which without any foreign person, of itself beautified itself,[69] and received her Grace at all places as hath been before mentioned, with most tender obedience and love, due to so gracious a Queen and sovereign lady. And her Grace likewise of her side in all her Grace's passage showed herself generally[70] an image of a worthy Lady and Governor. But privately these especial points were noted in her Grace, as signs of a most prince-like courage, whereby her loving subjects may ground a sure hope for the rest of her gracious doings hereafter.

*Certain notes of the Queen's Majesty's great mercy,
clemency, and wisdom used in this passage*

About the nether end of Cornhill toward Cheap, one of the knights about her Grace had espied an ancient citizen, which wept and turned his head back, and therewith said this gentleman, 'yonder is an Alderman,' (for so he termed him) 'which weepeth and turneth his face backward. How may it be interpreted that he so doth, for sorrow or for gladness?' The Queen's Majesty heard him and said, 'I warrant you it is for gladness.' A gracious interpretation of a noble courage,[71] which would turn the doubtful to the best. And yet it was well known that as her Grace did confirm the same, the party's cheer was moved for very pure gladness for the sight of her Majesty's person, at the beholding whereof he took such comfort that with tears he expressed the same.

---

[69] For this reference to the exclusion of foreigners from the entry pageants, see Introduction.

[70] To everyone; in opposition to 'privately' below, that is, among those attending her.

[71] The ancient physiology thought of the heart (Fr. coeur = heart) as the place where spirit was generated and stored; thus 'courage'= spirit, mind, disposition, nature.

In Cheapside her Grace smiled, and being thereof demanded the cause, answered for that she had heard one say, 'Remember old king Henry the Eighth.' A natural child, which at the very remembrance of her father's name took so great a joy, that all men may well think that as she rejoiced at his name whom this realm doth hold of so worthy memory: so in her doings she will resemble the same.

When the City's charge without partiality, and only the City was mentioned unto her Grace,[72] she said it should not be forgotten. Which saying might move all natural Englishmen heartily to show due obedience and entireness to their so good a Queen which will in no point forget any parcel* of duty lovingly showed unto her.

The answer which her Grace made unto master Recorder of London, as the hearers know it to be true, and with melting hearts heard the same, so may the reader thereof conceive what kind of stomach[73] and courage pronounced the same.

What more famous thing do we read in ancient histories of old time, than that mighty princes have gently received presents offered them by base and low personages. If that be to be wondered at (as it is passingly) let me see any writer that in any one prince's life is able to recount so many precedents of this virtue, as her Grace showed in the one passage through the city. How many nosegays did her Grace receive at poor women's hands; how oft-times stayed she her chariot when she saw any simple body offer to speak to her Grace. A branch of rosemary[74] given to her Grace with a supplication by a poor woman about Fleet bridge, was seen in her chariot till her Grace came to Westminster, not without the marvellous wondering of such as knew the presenter and noted the Queen's most gracious receiving and keeping the same.

What hope the poor and needy may look for at her Grace's hand, she as in all her journey continually, so her harkening to the poor children of Christ's Hospital with eyes cast up into heaven did fully declare, as that neither the wealthier estate could stand without consideration had to the poverty,[75] neither the poverty be duly considered unless they were remembered as being commended to us by God's own mouth.[76]

As at her first entrance she as it were declared herself prepared to pass through a city that most entirely loved her, so she at her last departing,

---

[72]It was pointed out to the Queen that all this was done by the city alone, and at its own cost.

[73]The stomach is still regarded as a seat of courage; we say 'I don't have the stomach for it.'

[74]Famously, of course, rosemary is for remembrance (*Hamlet* IV, 5: 175).

[75]The responsibility of the rich towards the poor.

[76]Matthew 5:3.

as it were, bound herself by promise to continue [a] good lady and governor unto that city which by outward declaration did open their love to their loving and noble prince in such wise, as she herself wondered thereat.

But because princes be set in their seat by God's appointing and therefore they must first and chiefly tender the glory of Him from Whom their glory issueth, it is to be noted in her Grace, that for so much as God hath so wonderfully placed her in the seat of government over this realm, she in all doings doth show herself most mindful of His goodness and mercy showed unto her, and amongst all other, two principal signs thereof were noted in this passage. First in the Tower, where her Grace before she entered her chariot lifted up her eyes to Heaven and said,

'O Lord, almighty and everlasting God, I give thee most hearty thanks that thou hast been so merciful unto me as to spare me to behold this joyful day. And I acknowledge that thou hast dealt as wonderfully and as mercifully with me, as thou didst with thy true and faithful servant Daniel thy prophet, whom thou delivered out of the den from the cruelty of the greedy and raging lions.[77] Even so was I overwhelmed, and only by thee delivered. To thee therefore alone be thanks, honour, and praise for ever. Amen.'

The second was the receiving of the bible at the Little Conduit in Cheap. For when her Grace had learned that the Bible in English should there be offered, she thanked the City therefor, promised the reading thereof most diligently, and incontinent commanded that it should be brought. At the receipt whereof, how reverently did she with both her hands take it, kiss it, and lay it upon her breast; to the great comfort of the lookers on. God will undoubtedly preserve so worthy a prince, which at His honour so reverently taketh her beginning. For this saying is true, and written in the book of Truth. He that first seeketh the kingdom of God, shall have all other things cast unto him.[78]

Now therefore all English hearts, and her natural people, must needs praise God's mercy which hath sent them so worthy a prince, and pray for her Grace's long continuance amongst us.

IMPRINTED AT LONDON IN FLEET STREET
within Temple Bar, at the sign of the
hand and star, by Richard Tottel
the twenty-third day of January.

---

[77] Daniel 6: 16–24.

[78] Matthew 6: 33 and Luke 12: 31; Elizabeth is referring to her earlier imprisonment in the Tower.

Appendix I
Contemporary Narratives of Elizabeth's Entry

1. Holinshed's depiction of the Thames on January 12
Raphael Holinshed, *The...Chronicles of England, Scotlande, and Irelande*. London: for John Hunne, 1577. STC 13568b. Vol. II, f. Rrrr^v (page 1788).

Compiling his *Chronicles* in the 1570s, Raphael Holinshed turned for his narrative of the entry itself to Mulcaster's 1559 pamphlet, but his brief account of her journey two days earlier by water to the Tower gives a vivid depiction of the way in which Londoners used their river on ceremonial occasions. This passage has some of the qualities of an eye-witness account, but Holinshed only arrived in London from Cheshire about 1560; his source may have been one of his collaborators on the *Chronicles*; William Harrison, for example, was a Londoner born.

On Thursday the twelfth of January, the Queen's majesty removed from her palace of Westminster by water, unto the Tower of London, the Lord Mayor and Aldermen in their barge, and all the citizens, with their barges decked and trimmed with targets* and banners of their mysteries* accordingly, attending her Grace.

The Bachelors' barge of the Lord Mayor's Company, to wit the Mercers, had their barge with a foist,* trimmed with three tops* and artillery aboard, gallantly appointed to wait upon them, shooting off lustily as they went, with great and pleasant melody of instruments, which played in most sweet and heavenly manner. Her Grace shot the bridge[1] about two of the clock in the afternoon, at the still of the ebb, the Lord Mayor and the rest following after her barge, attending the same, till her majesty took land at the privy stair at the Tower wharf, and then the said Lord Mayor with the other barges returned, passing through the bridge again with the flood, and landed at the wharf of the Three Cranes[2] in the Vintry.

2. The *Diary* of Henry Machyn (1559)
The Diary of Henry Machyn, Citizen and Merchant-Taylor of London, from A.D. 1550 to A.D. 1563. Edited by John Gough Nichols. Camden Society, no. 42 (London: 1848), 186–189.

Henry Machyn was probably a furnisher of funeral trappings, so the editor of his *Diary* surmises from the many funerals he reports. But Machyn also

---

[1] Passed underneath London Bridge at ebb tide.
[2] A tavern named after the cranes which lifted the vintners'* great barrels of wine; located just west of the northern exit of today's Southwark Bridge.

enjoyed public processions and displays of every kind. Some of his observations suggest he was still an adherent of the old religion. The manuscript of his *Diary* (BL Cotton Vitellius F. v.) was one of those damaged in the fire that consumed part of the Cottonian Library in 1731. This accounts for the number of conjectural emendations to the text which the nineteenth-century editor had to make; these are indicated in square brackets.

[The fourteenth day of January the Queen came in a chariot from] the Tower, with all the lords and ladies [in crimson] velvet, and their horses trapped with the same, and [trumpeters in] red gowns blowing, and all the heralds in their coat-armour[3], and all the streets strewed with gravel; and at Gracechurch Street a goodly pageant of King [Henry] the eighth and Queen Anne his wife and of their lineage, and in Cornhill another goodly pageant of King Henry and King Edward the sixth; and beside Soper Lane in [Cheap a]nother goodly pageant, and the conduit painted, [and] at the Little Conduit another goodly pageant of a quick* tree and a dead, and the Queen had a book given her there; and there the recorder* of London and the chamberlain delivered unto the Queen a purse of gold, full to the value of [blank]; and so to the Fleet Street to the conduit, and there was another goodly pageant of the two churches; and at Temple Bar was two great giants, the one's name was Gotmagot the Albion and the other Co(rineus).

The fifteenth day was the coronation of Queen Elizabeth at Westminster abbey, and there all the trumpets, and knights, and lordes and heralds of arms in their coat armour; and after all they in their scarlet, and all the bishops in scarlet, and the Queen, and all the footmen waiting upon the Queen, to Westminster Hall; there met all the bishops, and all the chapel[4] with three crosses, and in their copes, the bishops mitred, and singing *Salve festa dies*,[5] and all the street led with gravel, and blue cloth unto the Abbey, and railed on every side, and so to the Abbey to mass, and there her grace was crowned; and every officer ready against she should go to dinner to Westminster Hall, and every officer to take his office at service upon their lands;[6] and my lord mayor and the aldermen.

---

[3] The rich tabard or vest embroidered with the sovereign's arms, traditionally worn by the heralds.

[4] Presumably the chapel choir of men and boys.

[5] 'Salve Festa dies' ('Hail, festive day!'); text by Venantius Fortunatus (530–609). Unlike the 'Veni Creator Spiritus' and 'Te Deum' this is not one of the hymns specified for a coronation in the *Liber regalis*. The setting is unknown, but may have been that of John Sheppard (c. 1515–1560?) who was a member of the Chapel Royal at the time.

[6] Though feudalism was no longer a reality in England, its usages still influenced court custom. The noblemen who participated in the coronation banquet played roles assigned to them according to the feudal 'service' they were deemed to owe the crown, and they had to prove their right to do so in the days before the coronation.

3. The *Chronicle* of Charles Wriothesley (1559)

Charles Wriothesley, *A Chronicle of England During the Reigns of the Tudors, from AD 1485 to 1559*. Ed. W. D. Hamilton (Camden Society new series, vols. 11, 20, 1875–1877), 141–143. The original document was once among the papers of General Lord Henry H.M. Percy in the Staffordshire Record Office, which reports that it can no longer be located.

Charles Wriothesley (1508–1561) was Windsor Herald. His account of the entry itself is brief, but he gives a clearer picture than the other contemporary narratives of the religious and political circumstances in which it took place, and of the on-going ceremonial life of London. The marginalia of the original are not included; they merely point out the content of the main text. Dates and regnal numbers of monarchs have been normalized.

Philip and Mary, years 5 and 6.
Thursday the 17th of November, 1558, about six of the clock in the morning, Queen Mary died at her manor of St. James by Charing Cross.

And that day at eleven of the clock in the forenoon the Lady Elizabeth, her sister next inheritor to the Crown, was proclaimed Queen of England, France and Ireland, Defender of the Faith, etc. in London, with heralds of arms and trumpeters, etc.

Elizabeth. Year 1.
Friday the 18th of November Dr. Reginald Pole, Cardinal and Archbishop of Canterbury, died at Lambeth, in the morning, and was afterwards buried at Canterbury, in Christ's Church.

Wednesday the 23rd of November Queen Elizabeth came from Hatfield to the Lord North's house in the late Charterhouse* in London, the Sheriffs of London meeting her Grace at the further end of Barnet town,[7] within the shire of Middlesex, and so rode afore her till she came to Charterhouse gate, where she remained till the Monday after. Monday the 28th of November, at two of the clock in the afternoon, the Queen rode from the Lord North's house, along the Barbican, and in at Cripplegate, and along London wall to Bishopsgate, which was richly hanged, and where the waits of the City played, etc.

Monday the 5th of December the Queen departed from the Tower of London by water to her place by the Strand, called Somerset Place,* at ten of the clock in the forenoon, and went through London Bridge.

Tuesday the 13th of December the corpse of Queen Mary was honorably carried from the manor of St. James in the afternoon to the Abbey in Westminster. Her picture lying on the coffin apparelled in her royal robes, and a crown of gold on the head. And in the Abbey was a sumptuous and

---

[7]Today, a suburb of London. See Appendix II for their appointment on 19 November, 1558.

rich hearse* made, under which the corpse stood all night. And the morrow being Wednesday, after the mass of Requiem, the corpse were carried from thence to the new chapel, where King Henry VII lieth, and there in the side chapel, on the left hand, her corpse were buried for a time.[8]

Saturday 24th December was a solemn obsequy kept in the Abbey of Westminster for Charles V, late Emperor, who died in Spain in September last.[9]

Sunday the 1st of January the Lord Mayor and Aldermen gave in commandment to every ward within the City of London, that the parson or curate in every parish church in London should read the Epistle and Gospel of the day in the English tongue in the mass time [i.e., during mass]; and the English procession[10] now used in the Queen's chapel, according to a proclamation sent from her Majesty and her Privy Council, proclaimed in the City of London 30th December, which commandment was that day observed in most parish churches of the City.

Monday the 9th of January, in the morning, the image of Thomas Becket, which stood over the door of the Mercers' chapel in London toward the street, was found broken and cast down, and a bill set on the church door depraving the setters up thereof.[11]

Thursday the 12th of January the Queen's Majesty removed from her place of Whitehall to the Tower by water.

Saturday the 14th of January the Queen's Majesty at 2 of the clock in the aftenoon rode from the Tower through the City of London to her palace at Westminster, the Londoners having then made sumptuous provision of pageants and otherwise, as hath been accustomed.

Sunday the 15th of January the Queen's Majesty was with great solemnity crowned in Westminster Abbey, and after sat at dinner in Westminster Hall, which was richly hanged.

Wednesday the 25 of January the Parliament began at Westminster, the Queen's Majesty riding in her parliament robes from Whitehall to the Abbey, etc.

---

[8]Mary I is now buried beneath Elizabeth's well-known monument in the Lady Chapel of Westminster Abbey.

[9]European rulers, whatever their religion, paid close attention to the courtesies required by the births, marriages and deaths of their fellow-monarchs, regularly sending ambassadors to congratulate and condole on such occasions.

[10]By extension from its original usage (i.e., "in procession"), a litany, form of prayer, or office.

[11]Depraving, that is defaming or censuring. St. Thomas Becket had been a firm supporter of papal power. The hall and chapel of the Mercer's Company was built on land bought from a monastery erected on the site of the saint's birth.

4. Aloisio Schivenoglia reports to Sabino Calandra, Castellan of Mantua, 23 January 1559.

Mantua: Archivio di Stato, Archivio Gonzaga, busta 578, ff. 220r–230r, revised version of *Calendar of State Papers Venetian*, VII, 12–15 (see Textual Note).

Don Aloisio Schivenoglia ("Il Schifanoia" as he is usually referred to), was an Italian in the service of Sir Thomas Tresham, Prior of the Order of St. John of Jerusalem in England. At the time of Elizabeth's coronation there was no Venetian ambassador accredited to the English court, but the letters Schivenoglia wrote to Sabino Calandra and other Italians between 17 December, 1558 and 27 June, 1559 gave Northern Italians an absorbing eye-witness report of events during the transition from the reign of Mary to that of Elizabeth.[12] The selection presented here covers only the royal entry, and not his lengthy accounts of the ceremony of creating Knights of the Bath or the coronation itself. Nevertheless, it remains the first complete translation of this part of a narrative that is frequently cited.

Schivenoglia seems to have made some use of Mulcaster's text of the *Queen's Majesty's Passage*; for example after the events at the Little Conduit he is more indebted to the pamphlet and to hearsay. However, the two narratives are very different; among the functions of the Castellan of Mantua (governor or constable of the Castle of San Giorgio) was the organization of court festivities,[13] and this may be why Schivenoglia tells Calandra so much about the order of participants in the entry, their rank and dress, and also why he omits the "welcome" offered at Fenchurch Street and some passages of Latin verse. Because of its focus on ceremonial arrangements Schivenoglia's letter presents a court-centred view of such rituals – or at least the view of someone accustomed to European courts. It thus contrasts strongly with Mulcaster's pamphlet, which belongs so evidently to the civic culture of mid-sixteenth-century London. Schivenoglia was clearly much impressed by the richness and display of the English court, but he was disdainful of the Protestant imagery and propaganda of Grafton and Mulcaster's pageants.

[f. 220r–v] Her Majesty, wishing to follow the procedure of her ancestors for the Coronation, decided it would take place on the 15th of January of this year, 1559. She left her palace called Whitehall at Westminster on Thursday the 12th to go to the Tower by water. Ships, galleys, brigantines, caravels, barges and skiffs had been prepared with the most elaborate decoration possible of flags, artillery, drums, fifes, trumpets and other kinds of joyful instruments to accompany her Majesty and her court to the said Tower along the river Thames, so that it really resembled what one is accustomed to [see] on Ascension Day at Venice, when the Signoria goes to espouse the sea.[14]

---

[12] See Bellorini, 'Da Londra a Mantova: immagini di vita e cultura inglese nella corrispondenza di Aloisio Schivenoglia (1556–1560).'

[13] For Sabino Calandra and his relatives as devisers of court festivals, see Mitchell, *Italian Civic Pageantry in the High Renaissance*, 71–72, 75.

[14] The Ascension Day festival in Venice commemorates a victory in 997 by which

104   The Queen's Majesty's Passage

When the time had come that the tide made it possible to pass easily [under] London Bridge, which was about two hours after midday, her Majesty, accompanied by many knights, barons, ladies, and by the whole court, passing through the private corridor, embarked in her barge, which was covered with its usual tapestries, both inside the cabin and outside. The barge was pulled by another, a little less than a small galley in length, with forty men in shirts who rowed it in the fashion of a galley, and there were drums and fifes, as is the custom when she goes by water. After her Majesty passed the bridge and was in sight of the Tower some pieces of artillery were fired; in this way she landed at the private stairs, and entering by a little private bridge, was seen only by very few persons.

[There follows an account of the ceremony making Knights of the Bath on January 13, ff. 220v–223r. The description of the entry itself then begins:]

[f. 223r–230r] On the morning of Saturday the 14th, as after dining her Majesty was to make her state entry into London, everyone attended the Court in their best dress, and on horseback if they could, that is barons as well as knights, and also the ladies who were all dressed in crimson velvet with various linings, given as livery by the Queen, with such necklaces, gold on their heads, and jewels, that they made the air clear, though it was snowing a little.[15] While everyone was arriving the Queen and the entire court dined. The masters of munitions, with the gunners, arranged the artillery in order, some of it around the walls and with the big pieces outside on the piazza. Between the little and the big ones there were more than four hundred to make a fine salute as her Majesty departed. In the same manner everyone for his part decorated his house in the best way he could, from Blackfriars to St. Paul's, which is almost a long mile.[16] Along the streets there were wooden barricades on which the merchants and artisans of every trade leant in long black gowns with linings, their hoods of red and black cloth thrown back, like those usually worn by the rectors of universities in Italy. All their ensigns, banners, and standards, which were innumerable, made a very fine show. Owing to the deep mud caused by the foul weather and by the multitude of people and of horses, everyone had placed sand and gravel in front of their houses.

Venice gained control of Dalmatia; from 1177 onward it included a ceremonial marriage of Venice and the sea enacted by the Doge in the great barge the Bucintoro.

[15]The Arabic magical work *Picatrix* gives instructions for warding off thunderstorms with a bright mirror (and loud shouts); see Pingree, ed. *Picatrix*, 209. Schivenoglia and his friends must have known its Latin translation or one of the alchemical works referring to it.

[16]The length of a mile (theoretically 1000 Roman military paces) varied from country to country; that of Germany was notoriously long.

One cannot describe the order of the cavalcade very well because nobody kept his place, nor could they do so because of the multitude of people. However, it was as follows: after dinner, at two o'clock, the heralds began to marshal and order the others according to their rank, and two of them went ahead, making way. All were on horseback, wearing their accustomed ceremonial garb. The gentlemen followed, and knights of every sort mixed together, some on middling chargers and some on good hackneys and nags, some dressed in good-looking livery, some gracelessly and badly put together, so much so they made one laugh, others in their silk-lined garb, almost in our style, with chains and collars and gold points.* Then followed the chancellors, which is what they call here the clerks of the Great and the Privy seal,[17] with those of the Council, and afterwards the secretaries, other officials, the former councillors of the deceased queen, and the chaplains of Her Majesty, dressed in long robes of scarlet. After the abbot of Westminster, and the six bishops who were here, came the barons, that is the lords without title, and the gentlemen of the council. Then the viscounts, counts, dukes and marquesses, not observing their place because the great part of them were otherwise occupied.[18] Last in order came the count of Feria,[19] between the archbishop of York who had been the great chancellor, and he who currently guards the Great Seal until the creation of a new chancellor. After [this came] the sixteen trumpets of her Majesty, dressed in scarlet and blowing their horns, with the twelve mace-bearers in their places. Then came two knights in the ducal garb of former times, who carried in their hands two crowns, the one of iron and the other of gilded silver, along with the King of Arms,[20] who carried her Majesty's royal crown of gold. The earl of Arundel followed, grand steward of the kingdom, beautifully dressed on a charger very richly adorned, with the mayor of London, who carried the small regal sceptre, and the duke of Norfolk, with the silver baton of his office. There must have been 1000 horses in all. And last of all came her Majesty in an open litter, trimmed down to the ground with gold brocade with a raised pile, and carried by two very handsome mules covered with the same fabric, and surrounded by a multitude of footmen[21] in crimson velvet jerkins, all studded with massive gilt silver, with the arms of a white and red rose on their breasts and backs, and with two letters on either side, E.R., which signified Elizabeth Regina wrought in relief, the usual livery of this Crown,

---

[17]The chancellors of European courts originated as clerks or secretaries. In England the office developed into one of great estate; the Lord Chancellor, guardian of the Great Seal, is the highest officer of the crown. The office, probably the oldest senior government post in the world, is reportedly to be abolished.

[18]That is, had other roles in the procession.

[19]The ambassador of Spain; see Introduction.

[20]A herald, one of those associated with the Royal College of Arms.

[21]These footmen would be whifflers, guards armed with javelins or staffs whose business it was to clear the way.

which makes a most superb show. They were uncovered, and without anything on their heads.[22] At the sides walked the Gentlemen of the Axe, as the Pensioners are called,[23] with their hammers in hand, and clad in crimson damask, given them by the Queen for livery, all on foot and bareheaded.

Her Majesty was dressed in a very rich royal mantle of gold with a double-raised stiff pile, and on her head over a coif of cloth of gold, beneath which was her hair, she wore the plain gold crown of a princess, without lace but covered with jewels, and with nothing in her hands but gloves. Behind the litter came Lord Robert Dudley, Master of the Horse, mounted on a very fine charger and leading by the hand a white hackney covered with cloth of gold. Then came the great Lord Chamberlain and other lords of her Majesty's Privy Chamber, who were followed by nine pages dressed in crimson satin on very handsome chargers richly caparisoned, with their Governor and Lieutenant. After this [came] four carriages, in the shape of narrow litters, with high canopies on four little columns, two decorated with crimson velvet and two of scarlet with fringes of gold, and of silk of the same color. These were drawn by four chargers similarly decorated; they were so small that they did not hold more than four ladies each. In the first were duchesses [and] marquises, and the rest were arrayed according to their rank. Then followed perhaps forty ladies, gentlewomen and maidens of the Court dressed as above [in margin: on hackneys], and with caparisons of crimson velvet, and each was attended by a wiffler, very well dressed. That is, except for eight [ladies who] were dressed in cut velvet of pure crimson; and all had headcoverings of black velvet, with so much gold and jewellery that it was stupefying. Last came Her Majesty's guard of 100 very fine archers, all on foot following their captain, all dressed in a doublet of red cloth with two large stripes of black velvet four fingers wide, and two narrow sashes tied around the skirts of their doublets, the breast all embroidered with brocade of gilded silver in the fashion described above for the wifflers, but with a different pattern, which made a very beautiful show, with the pink crown, and letters, just like [those described] above. Each of their outfits could not have cost less than 100 *scudi*.[24] And in fact after that great solemnity they were never worn but were kept in the Wardrobe.[25]

Her Majesty then set off, and first passed the piazza of the Tower. The artillery began to fire, which went on for half an hour until her Majesty arrived

---

[22]Schivenoglia takes particular care to note when people did or did not uncover their heads; he seems to feel this mark of respect is not sufficiently employed by the English.

[23]The Gentleman Pensioners were the Queen's private guard; the position was chiefly honorary and was often filled by men of rank.

[24]The gold *scudo* of Florence was worth about six English shillings.

[25]The King's Wardrobe, a considerable department of the household, was in Carter Lane south of St. Paul's.

at Gracechurch Street[26], where the Londoners had raised the first triumphal arch, which was very lofty, divided into three levels. On the first were King Henry VII, of the House of Lancaster, with a large white rose in front of him, and Queen Elizabeth his wife, of the House of York, with a similar large rose in front of her, but red, [both] in royal robes. On the second level above there were seated King Henry VIII, with a similar rose in front of him, but white and red, [then] a pomegranate in the middle, and Queen Anne Boleyn, mother of this Queen, with a white eagle and a gold crown on its head and gilt sceptre in its right talon, the other resting on a little hill, and surrounded by small branches with little roses in front, the coat of arms and device of the said Queen. Further up on the third [level] sat a Queen in majesty to represent the present one, who is descended from the aforesaid. Outside, and higher still on the facade were the royal arms of England, trophies, festoons, etc. The arch had three vaults and three entrances, two small and a great one, with columns, capitals, and bases, etc. Above the two little doors, in a table on one side, were written in English, and on the other side in Latin, the following verses:

Hi, quos jungit idem [word missing in manuscript] *quos annulus idem...*[27]

On her Majesty approaching the aforesaid arch a boy came out on a little place for standing above the centre door, and briefly explained the whole subject of the allegory, and her Majesty stopped and gave him most grateful welcome, showing much satisfaction. Then going on her way and turning into Cornhill, having passed the first water conduit, which was painted with the royal arms and those of London, and [with] English and Latin mottoes, a little farther on she came to the second arch, no less handsome than the first, but not so so large or so high, with a very extravagant allegory, purporting [to say] that up to now religion and the government of the people had been badly understood and arranged, and that now things would be better, which was signified by a queen who sat on a high throne. On one side there were many persons clad in various fashions, with labels inscribed Religio Pura; Justicia Gubernandi, Intelligentia; Sapientia; Prudentia; Timor Dei. On the other side, alluding I suppose to the past, were Ignorance, Superstition, Hypocrisy, Vainglory, Simulation, Rebellion, and Idolatry etc. Likewise, the arch had three doors, on the two smaller of which were written in capital letters in English and Latin the following verses:

Quae subnixa alte solio Regina superbo est...

---

[26]Schivenoglia omits the welcome at Fenchurch Street, along with its verses.

[27]For complete versions of the Latin passages see the text of the entry; for translations, see Appendix III. Schivenoglia quotes them, probably from the pamphlet, with a few unimportant variations.

[As the queen passed] beneath the arch, an interpreter briefly explained the whole to her Majesty, as at the first arch. Then following the route, and entering Cheapside near the church of St. Thomas, after passing the fountain, which has been freshly repainted with arms, labels, and mottoes newly prepared in English and Latin, she encountered the third arch with the eight beatitudes described by the evangelist Matthew, chapter V, all of which they desire her Majesty to possess, with the following verses on the sides in Latin and English:

> *Qui lugent, hilares fient. Qui mitia gestant...*

Likewise her Majesty was briefly informed about this arch and its meaning, as she had been of the others. Going forward, she found herself at the Little Conduit, with a small tower having eight fronts, known as the Standard, and on it there were painted to the life all the kings and queens in their royal robes, with their dates and how long they reigned, down to this Queen. After a short distance she came to the great cross located in the middle of the street, built in the fashion of a pyramid, completely gilt and recently renovated, with all the saints in relief that are on it neither altered nor diminished.[28] Coming to the end of that street she encountered the aldermen, dressed in long robes of scarlet with very large gold neck-chains, and a *becca* or stole of black velvet at the neck; [there] she was presented with a purse containing 1,000 gold marks, that is, 2000 ducats. A very short speech was recited by the Recorder of London.

At the end of the said street facing the conduit they had built the fourth arch, with two hills on it, separated a bit from each other. [One was] green, flourishing and fruitful, the other dry, sterile and uncultivated. On the summit of the green one there sat a handsome youth, well dressed, joyous, and jocund, under the shade of a green laurel. On the dry one sat another youth dressed in black velvet, melancholy, pale and wan, under a completely dry and arid tree, loaded with labels and mottoes indicating the cause of its dryness and sterility, while on the green hill, in contrast, they showed the cause of its fertility and vitality. Between the two hills there was devised a grotto with a little doorway from which, when her Majesty arrived, an old man came forth scythe in hand, representing 'Time,' with his daughter 'Truth' at his side, and expressed a wish to mow and reap the grass on the pleasant mount. [This was] an allusion to the motto on the money heretofore coined by Queen Mary, her Majesty of holy memory: *Veritas temporis filia*. The whole implied in their tongue that the withered mount was the past state, and that now the green one had appeared, along with the time for gathering the fruits of truth as in the verses in Latin and English on both sides of the arch, which were these:

---

[28] That is, unchanged as a result of the alteration of religion.

Ille videns falcem laeva quam sustinet uncam...

On the left side of the aforementioned arch there was a little rest in the form of a preacher's pulpit, from which a small boy explained to her the whole meaning of the two hills, presenting her Majesty with a book generally supposed to be the New Testament in English [which the Queen took in her arms and embraced handsomely,[29] returning thanks, etc.].[30] Her Majesty then turned towards St. Paul's churchyard to enter Fleet Street, passing the City school[31] [where the students made her the following oration and then the gate][32] of Ludgate, where the prisoners of the Mayor of London are held. There were certain verses in Latin in praise of her Majesty above a little table, hanging at the front of the said gate, which was entirely painted with the arms of the City. I hear that she pardoned all those prisoners who were merely debtors.[33] [The procession] then entered the aforementioned part of the street [where] there was built on the first conduit a very graceful arch, with two little pyramids on the sides and a single level in the middle with a great door. On that level there sat, under a palm, Deborah with the Council of the Jews on the side, as one can read in the book of Judges, chapter 4, and in the tables of the said arch on both sides were written, in Latin and in English, the following verses:

Quando dei populi canaam Rex pressit Jabem...

When her Majesty had heard from the expositor the meaning of this arch, she passed directly to the gate of London that divides the Londoners from the [dwellers in] the suburbs, encountering first a platform with six levels, laden with the poor from the orphanage, who were more than 300 in number, dressed all alike in gowns of serge. The biggest was no more than twelve years old. They all made reverence to her Majesty, with a very brief little oration recommending themselves, etc. She then arrived at the said gate, at the sides of which were two statues of giants, that held up a table where was written in Latin the following verses, which briefly declared the meaning of the five arches that had been passed, in this fashion:

Ecce sub aspectu iam contemplaberis uno...

---

[29]Ital. 'nettamente.' Not current in modern Italian. Florio's *A Worlde of Wordes* (1598), 239, defines it as 'neatly, cleanly, purely, finely, handsomely,' and (interestingly in view of Schivenoglia's anti-Protestant views) 'smugly.'

[30]The material in square brackets was inserted above the line.

[31]That is, St. Paul's School. The Latin oration at St. Paul's, "Philosophus ille divinus Plato..." was included as a separate item (ff. 235r–v) at the end of the account of the coronation, along with the verses beginning "Anglia nunc tandem plaudas, lætare, resulta;" that material is in a different, or at least more formal, italic hand.

[32]The material in square brackets was inserted above the line.

[33]This episode is not reported in Mulcaster's pamphlet.

Thus continuing her passage, the Queen went to her palace of Whitehall in Westminster, which she found decorated with the richest and finest tapestries and hangings, as one would have expected for such a festivity. This entry went on from dinner time till night. After dinner, there was a little dancing, and her Majesty quickly retired, having to go to the coronation at an early hour. And thus everyone that evening went to prepare for the said ceremony.

5. Richard Grafton, *Chronicle* versions of the entry (1563, 1570)

Richard Grafton, *An abridgement of the Chronicles of England, gathered by Richard Grafton, citizen of London, Anno Do. 1563*. London: Richard Tottel, 1563 (STC 12148), 165v–167v.

Paralleling this text is the expanded description of the pageants from *Grafton's abridgement of the chronicles of England. Newly and diligently corrected and finished the last of October 1570*. London: Richard Tottel, 1570 (STC 12151), 178v–179r.

Some differences between editions are reported in the footnotes, including a few further revisions made in the 1572 edition.

For Richard Grafton's important role in staging Elizabeth's entry, see the Introduction. Here he appears as chronicler of the very events in which he took part. Grafton published historical chronicles as early as 1548, when his edition of Edward Hall's *The union of the two noble and illustrate famelies of Lancastre and Yorke* appeared. Though he ceased operations as a printer in 1553, issuing only a *Book of Common Prayer* in 1559, he continued to publish and revise his own historical chronicle throughout the 1560s; the last version was issued in 1572, the year of his death. The reasons for his 1570 expansion of the description of the entry pageants are debatable; was it an attempt to drive home the Protestant themes of the entry (especially the Queen's relationship to her 'estates'), a casual expansion of material in which he had renewed his interest, or perhaps even intended to catch the eye of the pageantry-loving Robert Dudley, earl of Leicester, to whom the Grafton *Chronicles* had regularly been dedicated?

After the decease of Queen Mary (whose government as before appeareth) was not so much disliked of many, as it was condemned almost of all, as well for the severity and shedding of much innocent blood, as also for the waste and spoil of the treasure of this realm, the loss of Calais, and making strangers* over-privy to the state and secret affairs of the same,[34] God (the father of all goodness) having compassion upon this realm at the earnest prayers and petitions of some good people, and when it was seen most to his good pleasure, did in the place of the said Queen Mary send unto us the most merciful Lady, named the Lady Elizabeth our redoubted* sovereign

---

[34]An allusion to Mary's Spanish marriage.

lady,[35] second daughter to the renowned and most famous prince King Henry the eighth and sister to the godly king Edward the sixth and also to the last Queen Mary, to reign over us;[36] whom the same almighty God hath by special miracle preserved in her innocency from the malice, spoil, and danger of her extreme enemies. And so the said noble, virtuous and merciful Lady took upon her (as of right unto her appertained) the regal government of the crown and realm of England and was proclaimed with sound of trumpet at Westminster, and in the City of London the seventeenth day[37] of November, the year of Christ 1558, Queen of England, France and Ireland, defender of the faith, etc. to the great joy and comfort of the people that heard the same. At the which proclamation were such sounds and rejoicing of the people with bonfires and banquets of friendly neighbours in the streets as before that time hath been seldom seen.

Shortly after this proclamation the Queen's Majesty, being then lodged at her former private house of Hatfield, came from thence to the City of London and rested in the house of the Lord North, which sometime was called the Charterhouse, and from thence removed to the Tower of London, where she remained until the fourteenth day of January next following, at which time she passed through the City of London toward her coronation.

In this mean time the Mayor and citizens of London, having intelligence of the day and time appointed for her highness's passage through the City, did beautify the same. And when the day of her passage was come,[38] her highness being placed in her chariot within the Tower of London, lifted up her eyes to heaven and said:

O Lord Almighty and everlasting God, I give thee most hearty thanks that thou hast been so merciful unto me, as to spare me to behold this joyful day. And I acknowledge that thou hast dealt as wonderfully with me as thou didest with thy true and faithful servant Daniel the prophet, whom thou deliveredst out of the den, from the cruelty of the greedy raging lions; even so was I overwhelmed, and only by thee delivered. To thee therefore be only thanks, honour, and praise for ever, Amen.[39]

Then her Grace passed from the Tower through the City of London, which was adorned and decked with sundry pageants and sights, as a manifest declaration of the good wills of the citizens towards her Majesty, as in Gracious Street, Cornhill, Soper Lane end, the Little Conduit, and in Fleet Street.

---

[35] 1572 reads "sovereign and chief governor," evidence of the still-rankling issue of whether a female queen could rightly be termed a 'sovereign.'

[36] 1572: 'to reign over us' omitted.

[37] 1572: On Thursday, the seventeenth day.

[38] 1572 inserts 'which was the thirteenth day of January.'

[39] Grafton's text differs in only three places from the text of the pamphlet, which reads 'as wonderfully *and mercifully* with me'; 'greedy *and* raging lions'; 'to thee therefore *alone* be thanks.'

[1563]

The first pageant declared the long desired unity which by our most dread Lady is surely knit between us and the holy gospel and verity of our saviour Jesus Christ.

The second set forth before her eyes the seat of governance supported by virtues, which suppressed the vices and enemies of the same.

The third manifestly depainted the eight beatitudes mentioned in the fifth chapter of Saint Matthew's gospel, which justly was applied unto her highness.

The fourth contained the ruinous state of the realm, now by her Grace restored to the dignity of a flourishing commonwealth, and also how Time leading us a weary journey at length gave us the light of God's word by the hands of this our most gracious Queen.

The fifth compared the politic government of the worthy Deborah unto the present state of our most gracious Queen, who although she had reigned but a spark of time, yet she had at large set out in herself the full property of a good and virtuous governor.

[1570]

The first pageant was the marriage of King Henry the seventh with Elizabeth the daughter of King Edward the fourth, whereby the two houses of Lancaster and York were united together, which signified the conjunction and coupling together of our sovereign lady with the gospel and verity of God's holy word, for the peaceable government of all her good subjects.

The second was a seat royal, supported by certain virtues, and her Majesty being placed in the said seat, suppressed all kind of vices which lay under her feet, which signified that the right office of a prince was, and is, to advance virtue and suppress vice.

The third was a beautiful stage, wherein were placed the eight beatitudes mentioned in the fifth chapter of St. Matthew's gospel, which justly was applied unto her highness.

The fourth was a mountain with a cabin in the middest, and on the one side of this mountain grew all withered, old and decayed trees and fruits, and on the other side were all fresh flowers and beautiful trees and fruits. And out of the cabin came an old man whose name was Time, and he delivered to the Queen a Bible in English, to restore us to God's verity, and to put away all dregs of Papistry, that the mountain might become all fresh.[40]

The fifth was a seat royal, wherein was placed Deborah, a Queen of the Jews that ruled Israel eleven years, having about her all her counsellors to talk and consult of the state of the realm and benefit of the commonwealth. This was made to encourage the Queen not to fear though she were a woman; for women by the spirit and power of Almighty God have ruled both honourably and politiquely, and that a great time, as did Deborah, which was there set forth in pageant.

---

[40] 1572: had now once again restored into us God's verity, whereby the dregs of Papistry might be put away, and so the mountain might become all fresh.

And as she passed through Ludgate, one near unto her repeated the great charge that the City had been at, to whom she gave this worthy answer, that she well considered the same, and that it should be remembered. Also being humbly requested at the petition of the Mayor of London, who presented unto her Majesty in a purse one thousand marks in gold, that she would continue their good Lady, she gave answer that if need should be, she would willingly in their defence spend* her blood; these worthy answers showed forth the excellent heart of a noble princess.[41]

---

[41] 1570 adds: The next day after, her Grace was crowned at Westminster by Doctor Oglethorpe, then Bishop of Carlisle. 1572 adds to that: for at that time there was no Archbishop of Canterbury.

Appendix II
Documents Relating to the Queen's Entry, 1558–1559

This Appendix contains selections from the documentary records of Elizabeth's royal entry. Several are well-known, having been published before. However their juxtaposition here, in chronological order, illustrates very effectively the involvement of a wide range of interest groups in the celebrations of January 14, 1559. The records of the Aldermen of the City of London show how intricately the preparations for the Queen's procession were intermingled with the daily business of running the City of London. From them we learn the names and City companies of the very men who worked on the pageants. Also included are records produced by two court offices, that of the Master of the Revels and the Lord Chamberlain,[1] which give us many details of the dresses and fabrics used. Of great interest is the garb worn by Elizabeth during the entry and later depicted in the so-called 'Coronation Portrait' (see cover); the same dress had been worn by Mary I during her entry and was altered by the Queen's tailor, Walter Fyshe, to fit Elizabeth.[2] As might be expected the court records, though chiefly concerned with the coronation day itself, are particularly rich (the account for materials for Elizabeth's litter is three pages long) and often repeat details; fuller excerpts are thus beyond the range of this edition.

Personal names have been conservatively modernized; when in doubt, they have been transcribed as they stand in the manuscripts. Uncertain words and words supplied for clarity appear between square brackets. Dates are adjusted to treat the year as beginning January 1.

1) November 19, 1558: London's Court[3] of Aldermen calls a Common Council[4] to plan the Queen's entry.

London: Corporation of the City of London, Court of Aldermen, *Repertories*, XIV, 1558-1561, f. 90^v-91^r.

---

[1]The Lord Chamberlain was the chief financial officer of the Queen's personal household (as distinct from her political council). The Revels Office organized court entertainments of all sorts; the Master of the Revels was one of the Lord Chamberlain's deputies.

[2]See Introduction.

[3]Literally, the regular formal meeting of the Aldermen as a group.

[4]London was governed by a Lord Mayor, the twenty-six members of the Court of Aldermen, one for each ward who held office for life, and the 212 members of the Common Council, parish magnates who tended to hold office for some years; see also Introduction.

Common consilium two fifteens[5]	Item, it was agreed that there shall be a Common Council held here upon Monday next coming, at nine of the clock, for the granting of two fifteens for the present that is to be given to the Queen's majesty by the City at the time of her coronation and for the provision of wood and other necessaries for the commonality of the said City.
Parish clerks and minstrels	Item, the wardens both of the parish clerks and also of the minstrels of this City were here presently charged to call severally their whole fellowships together and to put themselves with all convenient speed in good and perfect readiness to do the best and most comely service that they can for the honour of the said City at the Queen's majesty's first coming unto the same.[6] And Master Altham, Master Malory, Master Marten and Master Rowe, Aldermen, were assigned by the Court to appoint their standings and places and to take order with them for their decent behaviour in the doing of their said service and to give them notice of the time thereof.
The Sheriffs of London to receive the Queen at her grace's first entry into Middlesex	Item, it was agreed that both Master Sheriffs of this City shall receive the Queen's majesty at the utter part of the shire of Middlesex whereof they be also Sheriffs at the time of her highness's entry into the same shire, in their coats of velvet with their chains of gold about their necks and white rods in their hands; which rods they must kiss and deliver them jointly to her grace, and receiving them back again from her grace. The order is that they must place themselves amongst the gentlemen and so ride forth before her majesty till she comes unto them [the Mayor and Aldermen] and then they [are to] to take their places with my masters the Aldermen.

2) November 21, 1558: The Common Council levies funds for the Queen's gift and the building of pageants.

London: Corporation of the City of London, Common Council, *Letter Book S,* f. 182ᵛ.

---

[5]That is, 2/15ths of the value of one's property.

[6]These preparations, as well as the following instructions to the sheriffs, probably relate to the events of November 23-28; see Introduction.

Two fifteens to be levied towards the city's charges at the Queen's highness's coronation.

At this Common Council it was ordered granted and agreed by the same that there shall be collected levied and gathered of the citizens and other inhabitants of this City two whole and entire fifteens with all convenient speed to be levied according to the ancient custom used in this city in that behalf, as well for the accustomed present to be given to the Queen's most excellent majesty at her highness's coming through the said City to her coronation as also for the furniture of diverse pageants and other necessaries for the honourable receiving of her highness in the same City.

3) December 7, 1558: The Court of Aldermen allocates responsibilities to the guildsmen.

London: Corporation of the City of London, Court of Aldermen, *Repertories*, XIV, 1558-1561, ff. 97^r-98^r. See figure 6.

Item. This day the worshipful commoners hereunder named were nominated appointed and charged by the whole court to take the charge, travail and pains to cause at the City's cost and charge all the places hereafter mentioned to be very well and seemly trimmed and decked for the honour of the City against the coming of our sovereign lady the Queen's majesty that now is[7] to her Coronation through the City, with pageants, fine painting and rich clothes of arras*, silver and gold in such and like manner and sort as they were trimmed against the coming of our late sovereign lady Queen Mary to her Coronation, and much better if it conveniently may be done. Whereunto, they agreeing granted to do their endeavours.[8]

Commoners[9] appointed to devise pageants against the Queen's Majesty's Coronation

That is to say:

Philip Gunter
Thomas Hunt } Skinners* } for the Conduit*
Thomas Bannister   in Cornhill
Myles Mordyng   and the Stocks*
John Traves, Merchant Taylor*

---

[7] Who is now the Queen.
[8] Agreed to do these tasks to the best of their ability.
[9] That is, members of the Common Council.

Roland Hayward Clothworker*
Richard Barnes Mercer* } for the Standard
Robert Offley Haberdasher* } in Cheap*
Richard Stockbridge Mercer

Geoffrey Walkeden Skinner
Clement Cornwall Ironmonger*
Thomas Pearson Scrivener* } for the Great Conduit
Henry Buckfold Girdler* } in Cheap
Thomas Marston Haberdasher
Francis Barnham Draper*

Thomas Pycket Grocer*
Robert Wygge Aurifex* } for the Cross[10]
John Jackson Founder* } in Cheap
Edward Gylberd Aurifex

Richard Buckland Haberdasher
Thomas Browne Haberdasher } for the Little Conduit
John Harrison Aurifex } in Cheap
Richard Grace Aurifex

Thomas Sponer Aurifex
John Hulson Scrivener
Richard Ferrer Grocer
William Mortimer Carpenter* } for the conduit in
John Craythorne Cutler* } Fleet Street
Laurence Taylor Cutler
Francis Barker [no occupation given]
Garrard Lee Draper

George Heaton Merchant Taylor
William Peterson Haberdasher } for Fenchurch
Richard Taylor Grocer
Thomas Castell Draper

Henry Nayler Clothworker
George Allen Skinner } for Ludgate
Thomas Nicoll Goldsmith
John Lacy Clothworker

---

[10]The 'Eleanor Cross' in Cheapside; see figure 11.

> William James Merchant Taylor
> Richard Tottel[11] Stationer*
> Giles Atkinson Merchant Taylor   } for Temple Bar
> Bartholomew Broskerby Scrivener
> Richard Browne Merchant Taylor

4) December 13, 1558: Appointing overseers for the pageants.
London: Corporation of the City of London, Court of Aldermen, *Repertories*, XIV, 1558-1561, f. 99^r.

Item this day Richard Grafton and Francis Robinson, Grocers, Richard Hilles, Merchant Taylor, and Lionel Ducket, Mercer, were assigned and appointed by the Court here to survey the doing and devices of all the other commoners of this city which are already appointed to make and devise such pageants in sundry places of this city against the Queen's Majesty's coming to her coronation, as heretofore hath been accustomed at the like time, and to reform, alter or add unto the same as they with the advice of such as they shall call unto them shall think good and to make report here the next Court Day by a plat* of all their opinions and doings therein, and then to understand here[12] what sum of money the City hath in a readiness toward the doing therein. *Pageants*

5) 13 December, 1558: Collecting the 'two fifteens.'
London: Corporation of the City of London, Court of Aldermen, *Repertories*, XIV, 1558-1561, f. 98^v.

At this Court it was ordered that all the collectors of the two fifteens lately granted by act of Common Council for the affairs at this present [time] of this City shall pay and deliver over the same in every ward of this City to the Alderman Deputy of the same ward and they [are] to pay it over to the Chamberlain at that [ward] and precepts shall forthwith be made out for the same ward accordingly.

6) December 15, 1558: Removing the fence around the Cheapside Cross.
London: Corporation of the City of London, Court of Aldermen, *Repertories*, XIV, 1558-1561, f. 102^r.

---

[11]The stationer Richard Tottel would issue Mulcaster's pamphlet of *The Queen's Majesty's Passage* on January 23, 1559.

[12]To be advised.

120   The Queen's Majesty's Passage

At this Court it was agreed that the pale now standing about the cross in Cheapside shall be clearly [i.e., entirely] taken away.

the pale* at the Cross in Cheapside

7) 17 December, 1558: 'Attending at the Cupboard.'[13]
London: Corporation of the City of London, Court of Aldermen, *Repertories*, XIV, 1558-1561, f. 102^v.

Commoners attending at the Cupboard at the Queen's coronation

Item, this day William Chelsham, Mercer, William Chyvall, Draper, Francis Robinson, Grocer, John Harrison, Goldsmith, Robert Wades, Fishmonger,* Thomas Bannister, Skinner, Henry Beacher, Haberdasher, Edward Lee, Merchant, William Dame, Ironmonger, William Gibbons, Salter*, Thomas Lowe, Vintner*, and Roland Hayward, Clothworker, were named and appointed by the whole Court to attend upon the Chief Butler of England[14] at the Cupboard upon the day of the Coronation of the Queen's Majesty according to the ancient liberties, franchises and customs which time out of mind have always been allowed amongst other liberties unto the citizens of this City of London at the like times of coronation of any king and queen of this realm.

8) December 21, 1558: the painters* refuse to help.
London: Corporation of the City of London, Court of Aldermen, *Repertories*, XIV, 1558-1561, fol. 103^v.

Pageants and Playne

Item: forasmuch as the Painters of this City did utterly refuse to new paint and trim the Great Conduit in Cheap against the Queen's Majesty's coming to her coronation for the sum of twenty marks,[15] it was therefore ordered and agreed by the Court held this day that the surveyors of the same shall cause it to be

---

[13] This was a position of honour; the guildsmen named were to assist the Chief Butler (see below) at the great banquet following the coronation.

[14] The hereditary Chief Butlers of England were the Earls of Arundel, but the actual conduct of the post seems to have been divided between that nobleman and a lower court functionary, who at this time was Edward Elrington, according to PRO E101/87/24 and E101/87/26; see Streitberger, *Court Revels, 1485-1559*, 9.

[15] It is not clear why the Painters refused to assist; the money offered may have been too little, or the conduit may have been too recently refurbished, or inter-Company tensions could have played a role. The mark was a 'money of account,' that is, a unit used in calculating value, rather than a coin; its worth was fixed at 13 shillings fourpence.

covered with cloths of arras and such other rich cloths as they can get and cause certain escutcheons* of the Queen's highness's arms to be seemly made and set upon the same, and David Playne head warden of the Painters was commanded to attend upon the said surveyors of the Conduit and the surveyors of all the other pageants of the City and to help them with his advice and workmen for reasonable wages to the best of his power whereunto willingly he agreed and promised so to do.

9) 21 December, 1558: Setting up scaffolds and marshalling the guildsmen.
London: Corporation of the City of London, Court of Aldermen, *Repertories*, XIV, 1558-1561, fol. 104[r].

Item, it was ordered and agreed that Richard Buckland, Haberdasher, shall cause the carpenter to set up the scaffold in Saint Dunstan's churchyard in Fleet Street for the children of the house of the poor[16] by the day and not be great[17] and that he see that he and his men do labour honestly and that he keep well the reckoning of those charges.	London and the poor
Item, it was agreed that the bachelors of the Mercers company shall be permitted to stand together in Cheapside, directly over against the members of the same company on the further side of the street there at the Queen's coming to her coronation.	Bachelors* of the Mercers Company[18]

10) 3 January 1559: Queen Elizabeth's warrant for the loan of costumes to Sir Thomas Cawarden, Master of the Queen's Revels.
Washington: Folger Shakespeare Library Ms. L.b.33.[19] See figure 8.

Elizabeth R. By the Queen
    Whereas you have in your custody and charge certain apparel as officer for our masques and revels, this shall be to will and command you immediately upon the sight hereof that you deliver or cause to be delivered unto John Gresham and John Elliot, citizens of our City of London, such and so much of the said apparel as they shall require for the setting forth of those

---

[16] That is, the children of Christ's Hospital.
[17] See that their charges not be great.
[18] The Mayor of London in 1558-59 was a Mercer, Thomas Leigh.
[19] Attention was first drawn to this and the next document by Bergeron, 'Elizabeth's Coronation Entry (1559): New Manuscript Evidence.'

pageants which be appointed to stand for the show of our City at the time we are to pass through the same towards our coronation. Wherein you shall use your discretion to deliver such parcels as may most conveniently serve their turn, and therewithall take less hurt by use; receiving also of the said Gresham and Elliot a bill subscribed by their hands whereby to charge them with the safe delivery and restitution of the said apparel. And these our letters shall be your sufficient warranty and discharge in that behalf. Given under our signet at our palace of Westminster the third of January the first year of our reign.

To our trusty and well-beloved
Sir Thomas Cawarden, Knight

11) January 13, 1559: The mercers obtain costumes from the Revels Office.

Washington: Folger Shakespeare Library, Ms. L.b.109.

The note indented* of such garments as are this present 13th of January 1558 [i.e.,1559] delivered by Sir Thomas Cawarden, knight, Master of the Queen's Revels, unto John Gresham and John Elliot, Mercers, to be redelivered the 16th of this present month of January next coming,[20] that is to say,
First, a kirtle* for a woman of yellow cloth of gold upperbodied with tinsel and sleeves of gold.[21]
Item, a red cloak lined with white sarcenet* and a cape of silver.
Item, a woman's garment of silver upperbodied with scallop shells.
Item, a man's gown of russet velvet.
Item, three garments of blue cloth of gold with sleeves of flat silver.[22]
Item, two long garments of cloth of gold with black tinsel sleeves and capes.
Item, two garments, long, of red satin striped with gold and sleeves of white cloth, gold and red.[23]
Item, a cloak of yellow cloth of gold turfed[24] with white, and a sword.
Item, a coat of flat silver.

---

[20]For a discussion of the garments and they way they were used, see Bergeron, 'Elizabeth's Coronation Entry (1559): New Manuscript Evidence.' He speculates (7) that the garments had to be returned promptly because they were needed immediately for a masque.

[21]Bergeron suggests that this garment, resembling in its cloth of gold the garments the Queen was wearing on the day, was intended for Deborah in the final pageant.

[22]Probably silver tinsel.

[23]Bergeron suggests that these were intended for the figures of Henry VII and Elizabeth in the first pageant of the uniting of the houses of York and Lancaster.

[24]'To turf' means to strip off, roll back or strip bare; here it may signify a yellow cloak with strips cut out through which the white could be seen, or perhaps lined with white.

Item, an Irish garment[25] of yellow cloth of gold and yellow sarcenet.
Item, four pair of buskins,* two pair of blue velvet and two pair of red bodkin* and one other pair of red bodkin.
Item, eight caps and hats of cloth of gold.[26]
Item, a white purse for a falconer.[27]
Item, a hobert.*
Item, two white garment[s] of silver lawn, white with sleeves of cloth of silver.[28]
Item, two jerkins of taffeta, changeable red and yellow,[29] guarded with cloth of gold.
[signed] by me, John Elliott, mercer.

13) Altering Queen Mary's dress to fit Elizabeth.

London: The National Archives (formerly Public Record Office). Records of the Lord Chamberlain's Office, LC 2/4/3, f.7. See figure 4, and for Elizabeth's dress, the cover.

The Even of the Coronation

The Queen's Majesty's Robes of Cloth of Tissue	Walter Fyshe the queen's majesty's tailor, for translating* of a mantle surcoat and kirtle of cloth of gold tissue with gold and silver of the queen's majesty's store the kirtle furred with powdered ermine about the skirts the rest lined with white sarcenet the kirtle being whole afore with a high collar and laced on both sides with sleeves with annelettes[30] hooks and eyes of silver and gilt. Price thereof 13s 4d

Item for buckram for the vents* of the same kirtle. Price 18d

William Jorden the Queen's majesty's skinner for translating and new mending of the furs of a robe of tissue. Price thereof 40s

---

[25] A popular kind of lady's mantle, typically looped over the shoulder. Examples can be seen in many portraits of the period; see Arnold, 'Jane Lambarde's Mantle.'

[26] Bergeron, 'Elizabeth's Coronation Entry (1559): New Manuscript Evidence,' suggests that these caps were intended for the children representing the beatitudes in the pageant at Soper's Lane.

[27] Bergeron expresses puzzlement at the falconer's purse and (below) the hobert or hawk. Mulcaster's account mentions neither bird, but the falcon was a device of Anne Boleyn and a mechanical one supplied one of the more spectacular effects of her 1533 royal entry. If a live bird was flown at Elizabeth's entry, it goes unmentioned in the pamphlet.

[28] Bergeron suggests that these garments were intended for Time and his daughter Truth at the Little Conduit in Cheapside.

[29] Showing different colours in different lights or from different angles.

[30] Small rings, possibly used to reinforce the holes for lacing, possibly for decoration.

Item for one timber[31] of ermines for the performance[32] of the same robes. Price thereof 26s 8d

Item for a thousand and three hundred pinks and powderings[33] for the said robes price the thousand 20d — 26d

Of the Queen's majesty's store at her palace of Westminster 4 yards of tissue the ground gold and tissue silver for performance of the said kirtle price the yard £4 — £16

Of the store in the Queen's majesty's Great Wardrobe 10 ½ yards sarcenet white for lining of the same kirtle and surcoat price the yard 6s 8d — 70s

Of the same store 4 ½ yards purple cloth of gold tissue for performance of the mantle and surcoat at 4 pounds — £18

Sum £42 17s 6d

De stauro [from the storehouse] £37 10s
De emptione [bought for the purpose] £5 7s 6d

14) January 17, 1559: Storing the pageant materials for another occasion.

London: Corporation of the City of London, Court of Aldermen, *Repertories*, XIV, 1558-1561, fol. 110ʳ.

Item, it was ordered and agreed that Master Chamberlain should cause all the pageants to be taken down with speed and to save as much of the stuff of them as may be to serve at another time.	'payments'

15) March 4, 1559: The Queen gives the promised alms to the poor, and Richard Mulcaster is paid for 'making of the book' of the pageants.

London: Corporation of the City of London, Court of Aldermen, *Repertories*, XIV, 1558-1561, f. 143ʳ. See figure 7.

Item this day the Queen's majesty's sub-almoner brought in and paid and by order of this Court to the hands of the Chamberlain ten pounds which her highness hath given toward the relief and comfort of the most poorest persons within the city's hospital.	The Queen's alms to the poor

---

[31] A package of 40 half-skins (i.e., 20 pairs) of ermine skins.
[32] That is, the making of the robes.
[33] Pinks: decorative eyelets or scalloping; powderings: sprinklings of decorative spots.

Item, it was ordered and agreed by the Court here this day that the Chamberlain shall give unto Richard Mulcaster for his reward for making of the book containing and declaring the histories set forth in and by the City's pageants at the time of the Queen's highness coming through the City to her coronation forty shillings, which book was given unto the Queen's grace.

Camerarius
[Chamberlain]
Mulcaster

Appendix III
Translations of Latin Passages

1) At Fenchurch Street, the City's welcome:

'Urbs tua quæ ingressu dederit...'

Requires no translation, since a version in sixteenth-century English precedes the Latin in the text.

2) At the upper end of Gracechurch Street, the pageant of the uniting of the two houses of Lancaster and York:

'Hii quos iungit...':

The Latin poem repeats the English one, but without the last four lines referring to the Wars of the Roses.

The sentences concerning unity:

'Nullæ concordes animos...':
No power overcomes spirits in concord.
Those who cause fear when united inspire fear when divided
Discordant spirits divide; those in concord unite.
Small things are increased with peace, but great things are destroyed in war.
Joined hands are stronger to carry the burden.
The concord of the citizens is like a bronze rampart for the kingdom.
Those who contend long, suffer longer.
Quarreling princes are the scourge of subjects.
A prince born to peace is not given to arms.
Plenty is the daughter of concord, peace her granddaughter.
A divided state gladdens its enemies.
Those who hold to the same thing hold longer.
A divided kingdom is easily ruined.
Arms vainly attack the harmonious city.
Agreement between peoples sustains faith, etc.

3) At the lower end of Cornhill, the pageant of the seat of worthy governance:

'Quæ subnixa alte solio...':
She who sits as queen upon the magnificent high seat,
The image of a holy prince, restores gentle things.
She whom civic love supports, wisdom confirms,
Justice makes lustrous, and religion blesses.

Vain superstition and ignorance with its dull countenance,
Lie trodden beneath true religion.
Just love of the king tames unbridled and rebellious spirits,
Crushes those who flatter and the insolent.
When a wise person rules the empire, Folly sits
In darkness, and her godhead shall be a vain honor.

4) At the end of Soper Lane, the pageant of the eight beatitudes:

'*Qui lugent hilares...*'
Those who weep shall be made happy; those who bear a meek
Heart shall alone reap many cultivated acres.
Who hungers and thirsts for justice shall himself be filled.
And divine law will permit the man pure of heart to see God Himself.
The Lord will have mercy on him who is merciful to others.
Whoever is peaceful is a son of God.
Whoever suffers on account of justice and
Is burdened in spirit shall gain the kingdom of Heaven.
To such men the Almighty promised earth, sea and stars,
And each of these men shall be blessed.

5) At the Little Conduit, the pageant of Truth and Time:

'*Ille, vides falcem...*'
This man thou seest, who holds the scythe in his left hand,
Is Time, and with him stands his daughter Truth,
Whom he had not seen a long time; her father
Drew from out the rock and placed again in light.
The sad fellow who sits to the left in untended field,
Who, encircled by sharp rocks rising high, expires,
Warns us by his appearance what the republic may be when it
Has been ruined; contrariwise, that lovely youth recognizable by his garment,
Teaches [what the republic may be] when it thrives in blessedness,
As does the laurel, flourishing with everlasting branch.

5) At St. Paul's School, an oration in Latin and certain verses:

'*Philosophus ille divinus...*'

That divine philosopher Plato left to posterity this most astute among many great and wise sayings: 'That republic shall be happiest whose prince is learned in wisdom and adorned with virtues.'[1] Why should not Britain applaud this, if it were truly said (as it seems it truly was)? Why should not the people show their gladness and joy? Indeed, why should not this day be

---

[1] Plato, *Republic* vii.

marked with a white stone (as they say)?[2] This day in which so noble a prince is come, whose like none before have seen, whom posterity can easily recognize, in all ways the happiest, gifted in both body and spirit. The gifts of a chaste body are so evident that they stand not in need of prayer, and those of the spirit, that they cannot be expressed by words. This woman, truly born of high kings, abounds in nobility of morals and spirit. In her breast burns the love of the faith of Christ. She shines with the virtues of the British people, and protects them with the shield of justice. Distinguished in Greek and Latin letters, she is surpassing as well in character. At her command, piety shall thrive, England flourish, the golden ages return. O all you English, now accept Elizabeth our most celebrated Queen, destined by Christ to the rule of this kingdom, and follow her with due honour. Submitting to her rule with freest spirit, you show yourselves worthy of such a prince. And since boys can fulfil their office not by strength but by prayers, we the pupils of this school built by Colet, once Dean of St. Paul's,[3] holding out young hands to Heaven, will pray to Christ the Greatest and Best, that He cause Your Highness to reign over the English with the highest honour for Nestor's years,[4] and with the dearest pledges[5] make you a happy mother. Amen.

> *'Anglia nunc tandem plaudas...':*
> England, now together, praise, rejoice, echo
> Your life is at hand, and your defence.
> In thy hope has come thy glory, light, all honour,
> Now she is come, who will surely bring strength
> She will aid in thy affairs, which were perishing.
> All things shall flourish, the golden ages now return.
> The good things that had fallen will rise up.
> Thou must then render all thy faith
> To her in whose accession you take such satisfaction.
> Therefore hail her from the bottom of your hearts.
> The health of Elizabeth's reign is undoubted,
> The virgin is come and, in turn, that we wish for shall come.
> With the sweetest pledges, she will come, happy parent.
> May Almighty God, from from highest Olympus,
> Grant this, he who created and rules Heaven and Earth.

6) At the conduit in Fleet Street, the pageant of Deborah:

> *'Quando dei populum Canaan...':*
> When Jaben king of Canaan oppressed God's people
> There was sent by great God, great Deborah

---

[2] See note 53 to main text.
[3] See note 54 to main text.
[4] See note 55 to main text.
[5] See note 56 to main text.

To free the people and save holy Judah,
To shatter the enemy's might with the army of her people.
This most happy woman, the Lord God ordaining,
Contended with the sword against [her] adversaries.
For forty years she reformed the people with justice,
Mighty in war, steadfast in peace.
Thus, O thus, Elizabeth, govern the people in war and peace;
Be a Deborah to thine English [people].

7) At Temple Bar, two poems, one describing the effect of all the pageants and the second a farewell from the City:

'Ecce sub aspectu...'
Behold, in one display thou seest them all,
O Princess, thy people's only pillar.
Whatever thou hast seen elsewhere in this vast city
This one arch demonstrates what all the rest comprehend.
The first gave thee, true heir to thy father,
To the throne of thy grandfather's realm.
When vices were suppressed and virtue reigned.
The second confirmed thy seat, O royal virgin.
The third set before thee [thy] blessed share
If thou shouldst persist in what thou hast begun.
In the fourth thy people showed thee truth, and what
The republic was when fallen, which stood when flourishing.
In the fifth great Deborah admonished thee,
Sent by Heaven to the long rejoicing of thy kingdom.
Go forth, O Queen, thy people's only hope,
Take with thee this, the city's vow.
Live long and reign long, O Queen,
Adorn thy father's state with virtue.
Hope of thy people, protect their cause.
Thus, O thus, is Heaven attained, thus the stars reached;
This is the work of virtue, all else shall be of death.

'O Regina potens...':
O mighty Queen, when first thou enteredst this city,
It gave thee as gifts tongues and loyal hearts;
Now as thou leavest, the city gives thee two gifts,
Prophesies full of hope and vows full of prayers.
For it is the hope of thy subjects
That thou shalt reign providing virtue,
Nor shall there be any place for error.
For it is the hope of thy subjects that thou shalt
Restore all truth, thou who shall restore
Good comfort, as thou takest away evil
Confident in this hope, they pray thou shalt long reign as Queen,
And exile from thy reign every criminal deed.

Confident in this hope, they pray that divine grace
The basis of true faith, should make thee strong.
Now, Queen, farewell; and one hope sustains us,
That error shall be destroyed, now that Truth is brought in.
This, then, we hope: that thou shalt be a gracious Queen
Unto us throughout thy long reign.

Glossary and Gazetteer

This list combines a glossary of difficult or obsolete words occurring in all the texts with a gazetteer of the London place names that are mentioned. Also listed are the City companies, since many of them still flourish today. Difficult words are marked with an asterisk where they first appear in a specific text. Longer phrases that require explanation in context are glossed in footnotes at the point where they occur. Some words defined here may also occur in the text with their ordinary modern meanings, for example 'noise*' means a band of instruments, but 'noise' (without an asterisk) means 'a loud sound.'

Historical material on London places is drawn chiefly from Stow's classic *Survey of London* (1603), Prockter and Taylor, eds., *The A to Z of Elizabethan London*, and articles in Weinreb and Hibbert, *The London Encyclopedia*. For a complete list of all the London Companies to 1995, with details of their ancient crafts and modern charitable activities, see 'City Livery Companies' in *The London Encyclopedia*; see also Herbert, *The History of the Twelve Great Livery Companies of London*. Information about more recently formed livery companies such as the 'Information Technologists' and 'World Traders' can be found on <http://www.englishorigins.com/help/LiveryCompanies.aspx>.

against. 1) Came up to, came abreast of; 2) until, in expectation of; 3) near, beside; 4) to, towards.
Armourer. Maker of armour and weapons; a member of the Worshipful Company of Armourers and (since 1708) Brasiers.
artificially. Skilfully, with art.
Aurifex. See goldsmith.
bachelor. A junior member, or 'yeoman' of a livery company. For today's bachelors, sometimes members of the Company of Young Freemen, see figure 5a.
base. Not of noble birth.
bodkin. Rich embroidered cloth with warp of gold thread and woof of silk; rich brocade or shot silk.
buskins. A low boot covering the foot and calf.
Carpenter. A member of the Worshipful Company of Carpenters.
charge. Expense, cost.
Charterhouse. The former abbey of the Carthusian monks near Smithfield Market, today Sutton's Hospital in Charterhouse, an almshouse for elderly gentlemen founded in 1611. Its often-reconstructed fabric forms part of the north border of Charterhouse Square, familiar as the location of the great detective's flat in the television series 'Poirot.'

Cheap, Cheapside. 'Cheap' means any market, but in London it specifically refers to the large market area, now a wide street, known as Cheapside, and still as prosperous as it was in 1559. 'The big salaries and huge bonuses paid to City workers makes the shopping street at the centre of the Square Mile the best in the British retail business, according to a new survey.' (*The Guardian*, July 20, 2001).

Clothworker. A finisher of woven woollen cloth. The Clothworkers Company was one of the 'Twelve Great' companies.

conduit. A public water pipe; cistern; fountain (and, consequently, a gathering place). The Great Conduit in Cheap, begun about 1285, was at the east end of Cheapside. The Little Conduit was built about 1442 at the west end, in front of St. Michael le Querne (see figure 13). The conduit in Fleet Street, at the head of Salisbury Court, was built 1453–1471. See also Standard.

Cutler. A maker of knives. a member of the Cutlers Company

device. An emblematic or heraldic design, usually with a motto.

Draper. A worker in woollen (and sometimes linen) cloth. The Drapers Company is one of the 'Twelve Great' livery companies and is still influential in City politics.

dread. To be feared and respected (adj.).

escutcheons. Shields painted with noble coats of arms.

Fishmonger. A seller of fish; a member of the Worshipful Company of Fishmongers, one of the 'Twelve Great' livery companies of London. The company is still active in regulating the fisheries.

foist. A small barge or ship's boat.

Founder. One who founds or casts metal, or makes articles of cast metal, particularly bells. A member of the Worshipful Company of Founders.

furnished. Apparelled, fitted out, equipped with, provided with.

furniture. Equipment, apparel.

Garter. The principal herald, Garter King of Arms.

Girdler. A maker of girdles or belts; a member of the Girdlers Company.

Goldsmith. Someone whose trade is working gold, both jewellery and plate; a member of the Goldsmiths' Company, which among other activities still operates the London Assay Office.

Grocer. One who trades in spices (especially pepper) and other luxury goods; a member of the Worshipful Company of Grocers, second in precedence among the 'Twelve Great' livery companies.

ground. Basis for exposition, foundation of the argument.

Haberdasher. One who sold ribbons, beads, purses, gloves, etc., and (after 1502) made hats; a member of the Haberdashers Company, one of the 'Twelve Great' livery companies.

Hatfield. Hatfield Palace is located 21 miles north of London's Charing Cross, in Hertfordshire. Built by the Bishop of Ely about 1497, it was taken over by Henry VIII as a home for his daughters; Elizabeth lived there in the years before her accession. Part of the Tudor palace was torn down by Burghley's son Robert Cecil when he built Hatfield House in the early seventeenth century.

hearse. A framework or platform for the candles and decorations surrounding the bier of a distinguished person; a catafalque.

hobert. Hawk.

incontinent. Straightaway, immediately.

indented. Literally, recorded in an indenture, a document bisected in a serrated pattern which the rightful parties to the agreement could reconstitute by comparing the wavy edges. More generally, a formal agreement.

Ironmonger. A worker in iron and steel; a member of the Ironmongers Company, one of the 'Twelve Great' livery companies.

jar. Jarring, quarrelling.

kirtle. Can mean a man's tunic, but most frequently means a woman's gown or skirt.

Mercer. One who exports and imports woollen cloth and luxury fabrics. The Mercers Company is first in precedence among the 'Twelve Great' livery companies. Though its trade connections have long been severed, its property holdings and charities still make it the most powerful of all the City companies.

Merchant Taylor. A tailor who also sells the materials of his trade. The Merchant Taylors' Company is one of the 'Twelve Great' livery companies of London. When Merchant Taylors' School was founded in 1561 Richard Mulcaster became its first Headmaster.

mystery. Craft or trade.

nether. Lower.

noise. A small band of musical instruments.

one. 'A' or 'an'; occasionally also means 'a person.'

pageant. Very loosely defined in studies of royal entries; see however 'pageant: 1) a portable image or device for parading at a public spectacle... 2) a play or tableau publicly acted in a stage or platform... 3) scenery and properties [?].'[1]

Painters. The Painter-Stainers (two companies amalgamated in 1502) painted signs and portraits and stained tapestries. Ralph Treswell, the surveyor whose depiction of the Little Conduit appears in figure 13, was a Painter-Stainer.

pale. Fence or barrier.

parcel. Portion.

penthouse. A light structure or awning built against the wall of a larger building

plat. A scenario, plan or map; (also) a platform.

points. Laces or cords for attaching the hose to the doublet.

portes. Portals or doors.

---

[1] *Bristol*, 335.

pretty. Well-adapted, well-made.
proper. Fitting, appropriate; (also) belonging to.
quick. Living.
rampant. An animal depicted in heraldry rearing or standing with its fore-paws in the air.
Recorder. The Recorder of London was appointed by the court of aldermen to make a record of the proceedings of their courts and the customs of the city. He was – and still is – the chief legal officer of the City of London, taking precedence in the Court of Aldermen over all who have not served as Lord Mayor.
redoubted. Feared or dreaded; reverenced, respected (usually of the sovereign).
regals. A small portable reed organ.
room. Space.
Salter. Salters imported and distributed salt, which was critical in preserving meat and fish; they also dealt in chemicals; a member of the Worshipful Company of Salters.
sarcenet. A soft, fine silk material.
scaffold. A raised platform erected for the presentation of a pageant or tableau.
Scrivener. One who wrote and copied legal documents (wills, charters, etc.) and latterly a notary. A member of the Worshipful Company of Scriveners, which continues to examine, admit and regulate Scrivener Notaries.
sentences. Sayings or mottoes.
several. Separate, different.
Skinner. One who prepares furs and skins for commercial use; a member of the Worshipful Company of Skinners, one of the 'Twelve Great' livery companies.
Somerset Place. Begun by Protector Somerset in 1547 but never finished. Edward VI assigned it to Elizabeth as her London residence. The great eighteenth-century building on the site today houses the Cortauld Institute Gallery, as well as a cultural centre.
spend (blood). Shed.
Standard, The. A fountain towards the west end of Cheapside, built about 1285; a gathering place where proclamations were often read.
standing. A small platform; a place to stand.
Stationer. A printer and bookseller, and thus a member of the Stationers Company, today the Stationers' and Newspaper Makers' Company.
Stocks. The Stocks was the old market at the intersection of Cornhill and Poultry; it was replaced between 1735–1752 by the Mansion House, residence of the Lord Mayor.
strangers. Foreigners.
table. A painted board, poster or paper sign.
targets. Shields, escutcheons.
tofore. Before

top. A platform on a ship's mast.
translating. Altering, re-cutting, refitting.
try, tried. Experienced.
vents. Pleats.
Vintner. A wine trader and member of the Worshipful Company of Vintners, one of the 'Twelve Great' livery companies.
void (void places, void room). Empty spaces.
wiffler. A guard armed with a javelin or staff who clears the way through a crowd.
weale. Health or well-being.

Textual Note

This volume contains a lightly modernized text of the single extant copy of what is believed to be the first edition of the pamphlet *The Quenes maiesties passage through the citie of London to westminster the daye before her coronacion.* published by Richard Tottel on January 23, 1559 (STC 7985.5).[1] *The Queen's Majesty's Passage*, as it is usually known, was quickly re-issued, bearing the same date in the colophon as the original publication. It was re-published in 1604, and even copied out by hand later in the seventeenth century. The text was included in Raphael Holinshed's *Chronicle* (1577 and 1587), quoted almost in full in John Strype's *Annals of the Reformation* (1708–1709), reprinted by John Nichols in *The Progresses and Public Processions of Queen Elizabeth* (1823) and by Thomas Allen in volume I of *The History and Antiquities of London, Westminster, Southwark and Parts Adjacent* (1827–1829), published in facsimile by the Yale Elizabethan Club in 1963, and reprinted in Arthur Kinney's anthology *Renaissance Drama, An Anthology of Plays and Entertainments* (1999). Over the centuries it has been much studied and quoted by scholars, though there has never been a full critical edition.

This new version does not pretend to be such an edition; for one thing, it presents a modernized text. However, exemplars of the known sixteenth and seventeenth-century versions have been compared with each other, and the apparent substantive variants (which are few) are indicated below.

In addition the text is accompanied by appendices containing a number of related documents, where possible transcribed from the originals. Appendix I collects five contemporary narratives of the occasion. Among them is a revised and more complete translation, based on the original manuscript in Mantua, of the account of Elizabeth's entry by the Italian observer Aloisio Schivenoglia, 'Il Schifanoia.' Appendix II reproduces a number of records relating specifically to the royal entry itself; there are many more documenting the coronation proper on the following day. The coronation was a religious ritual rather than a secular one, and its importance and rich historiography makes it a separate topic, one not touched on here. Appendix III provides English translations of the Latin passages in the entry.

---

[1]The title was entered to Tottel along with two others at an unspecified date between 10 July 1558 and 10 July 1559: 'Rycharde tottle ys lycensed to prynte *the passage of the quenes maiesties Throwoute the Cytie of London / The frute of foes* and a *treates of* senaca ijs iiijd,' Arber, *A Transcript of the Registers of the Company of Stationers of London, 1554–1640*, I, 96.

Modernization

The volume presents a lightly modernized text of the *Queen's Majesty's Passage*, the narratives in English (for Schivenoglia's account in Italian, see below), and the related documents. Spelling has been modernized, but older verb forms ending in -th have been retained. V/U and I/J have been normalized in the English text. The inconsistent capitalization of the original has been systematized; roman numerals are given as words (iiii = four). A few missing words necessary for the sense have been supplied in square brackets. Obsolete words appear with an asterisk at their first occurrence in a given text, and are explained in the *Glossary and Gazetteer*. Additional paragraphing has been introduced in a few places where it would aid the reader. In the Latin passages, U/V has been normalized and abbreviations have been silently expanded; thus, e.g., 'prim̄' becomes 'primum.' Occasional accent marks, e.g. 'quám' are not indicated. In the text of the Introduction quotations from early sources have also been modernized.

The Narrative of 'Il Schifanoia'

A version of Aloisio Schivenoglia's letter to Sabino Calandra, excerpted in Appendix I, was first printed in the *Calendar of State Papers: Venetian* (1890) where his name was given as 'Il Schifanoia.' Though that version of the document has been frequently cited, its transcription and translation have been severely criticised by Italian scholars.[2] Schivenoglia's letter is written in a clear cursive italic with some abbreviations. It has a few corrections and interlineations that indicate it was revised before it was sent, and the oration (not reproduced in this edition) at St. Paul's School was appended as a separate document. The 1890 CSPV version was selective; it included reports from Schivenoglia's letters of earlier festive events at court, but omitted extensive passages describing the ceremony of making Knights of the Bath, and the account, in which he was clearly very interested, of the garments and order of precedence in the entry procession itself. This translation contains the complete section covering the entry procession itself, omitting with regret as being outside the range of this edition the revelry at court in the days before the coronation, the creation of the Knights of the Bath on January 13, and the day of the coronation itself.

The translation is roughly based on the CSPV version, but wherever necessary it follows the Mantuan original; material omitted in CSPV has been re-inserted, the text checked closely against both the original manuscript and the printed text of the *Queen's Majesty's Passage*, and some free translations and out-dated wording in the CSPV text revised. Where the Latin verses are included, only their first lines are given here. Original paragraphing has been preserved, but sentences have sometimes been divided to clarify the sense.

---

[2] Luzio, 'I carteggi dell'Archivio Gonzaga riflettenti l'Inghilterra,' esp. 26–27. See also Bellorini, 'Da Londra a Mantova: Immagini di vita e di cultura inglese nella corrispondenza di Aloisio Schivenoglia (1556–1560).'

The Texts of The Queen's Majesty's Passage

There exist six early texts of *The Queen's Majesty's Passage* (listed here with the copies used for comparison):

A   *The Quenes maiesties passage through the citie of London to westminster the daye before her coronacion.* London: Richard Tottel,1559, with a colophon giving the date of publication as 23 January 1558 (i.e. 1559). STC 7985.5. Only known copy: Yale University: Beinecke Rare Book and Manuscript Library; Eliz. 157.

B   *The Passage of our most drad Soueraigne Lady Quene Elyzabeth through the citie of London to westminster the daye before her coronacion.* London: Richard Tottel, 1559, with a colophon giving the date of publication as 23 January 1558 (i.e. 1559). STC 7590. Huntington Library 31398.

C   Raphael Holinshed, *The...Chronicles of England, Scotlande, and Irelande.* London: for John Hunne, 1577. STC 13568b. Centre for Reformation and Renaissance Studies, Victoria University, University of Toronto. DA 130 .H74 1557a. Volume II, folios Rrrr.v[v]–Ssss.ii[v].

D   *The Royall Passage of her Maiesty from the Tower of London to her Pallace of White-hall, with all the Speaches and Deuices, both of the Pageants and otherwise, together with her Maiesties seuerall Answers, and most pleasing Speaches to them all.* London: S. Stafford for Jone Millington, 1604. STC 7592. British Library, C.33.e.7.(15).

E   *The Royall Passage of her Maiesty from the Tower of London, to her Pallace of White-hall, with all the Speaches and Deuices, both of the Pageants and otherwise, together with her Maiesties seuerall Answers, and most pleasing Speaches to them all.* London: S. Stafford for John Busby, 1604. STC 7593. British Library, C.33.e.7. (11).

F   Manuscript copy of B in an anonymous hand; mid-or late-seventeenth century. Yale University: Beinecke Rare Book and Manuscript Library; Eliz. 157A.

In 1960 James M. Osborn argued that A was the first edition, basing his discussion on several variants that he considered substantive.[3] However, a preliminary collation of A with an exemplar of B has shown that he was wrong about at least one of these; in A, Diii[v] very clearly reads 'staie' and not 'state.' As well, there are a number of differences between the texts that deserve future detailed examination.

Secondary evidence suggests that there may have existed a third early edition, now lost (X?). First, only C agrees with A at Eiii[r] ('all natural Englishmen'), but it differs from A elsewhere. Second, Aloisio Schivenoglia's narrative makes some use of Mulcaster's account, but his letter to Sabino

---

[3]Osborn, ed., *The Quenes Maiesties Passage through the Citie of London to Westminster the Day before her Coronacion*, 20–21.4

Calandra is dated January 23, the same date as that in the colophon of A and B. It is possible he began his letter on the day the pamphlet was published, but equally possible that he was using an earlier edition. Thus, though A probably precedes B, it is not absolutely clear that it is the first edition.

Based on a collation of one exemplar of each, it appears that B and D differ only in their title pages; both descend from B. Comparison of F (not known to Osborn) with the exemplars of B, D and E shows that F was copied from an exemplar of B. Such limited results are only suggestive, but it appears that earlier conclusions may need to be revised in the light of further study.

Variants

Bi^v A which so was, and every personage appointed B C D E F *omitted*
Biii^v A B C F which did tread their contrary vices under their feet D E *omitted, replaced with* Pure religion did tread upon Superstition and Ignorance *etc. (i.e., each virtue is described as separately treading down its contrary)*
[Cii^v]⁴ *A printed slip is pasted down, correcting Sir John Parrat's name*; B C D E F Sir John Parrat
Ciii^v A maister Parrat B C D E F Sir John Parrat
Eiii^r A al natural Englishmen B all Englishmen C all natural Englishmen D E all Englishmen F al Englishmen

---

⁴Cii is misnumbered as Ciii. Osborn regarded this as a substantive variant indicating the order of the two editions, but this is not necessarily the case.

Bibliography

Abbreviations:

CSPD. Calendar of State Papers Domestic. *Edward VI, Mary, Elizabeth, and James I*. Ed. R. Lemon and Mrs. Everett Green, 1547–1625.12 vols., London: HMSO, 1856–1872.

CSPV. Calendar of State Papers and Manuscripts Relating to English Affairs Existing in the Archives and Collections of Venice and in Other Libraries of Northern Italy. Vol. VII, 1558–1580. Ed. Rawdon Brown and G. Cavendish Bentinck. London: HMSO, 1890.

DNB. Dictionary of National Biography. Ed. Sir Leslie Stephen [and Sidney Lee]. London: Smith Elder and Co., 1885–1901.

STC. A. W. Pollard and G. R. Redgrave, with W. A. Jackson, F. S. Ferguson, and Katharine M.. Pantzer, eds., *A Short-Title Catalogue of Books Printed in England, Scotland, & Ireland*, second edn. 3 vols. London: The Bibliographical Society, 1986–1991.

Primary Sources

London: The British Library.
  The Royall Passage of her Majesty from the Tower of London to her Pallace of White-hall, with all the Speeches and Deuices, both of the Pageants and otherwise, together with her Majesties severall Answers, and most pleasing Speeches to them all. London: S. Stafford for Jone Millington, 1604. (STC 7592). C.33.e.7.(15).
  The Royall Passage of her Majesty from the Tower of London to her Pallace of White-hall, with all the Speeches and Deuices, both of the Pageants and otherwise, together with her Majesties severall Answers, and most pleasing Speeches to them all. London: S. Stafford for John Busby, 1604. (STC 7593). C.33.e.7.(11).

London: Corporation of London Record Office.
  Court of Aldermen, *Repertories*, XIV, 1558–1561.
  Common Council, *Letter Book S*, f. 182^v.

London: The National Archives (formerly the Public Record Office).
  Records of the Lord Chamberlain's Office: LC 2/4/3, f.7.

Los Angeles: The Huntington Library.
  The Passage of our most drad Soueraigne Lady Quene Elyzabeth through the citie of London to westminster the daye before her coronacion. London: Richard Tottel, 1559. STC 7590. Huntington Library 31398.

Mantua: Archivio di Stato di Mantua.
  Archivio Gonzaga, *busta* 578, ff. 216–234 (letters of Aloisio Schivenoglia).

New Haven: Yale University. Beinecke Rare Books and Manuscript Library.
The Quenes maiesties passage through the citie of London to Westminster the daye before her coronacion (London: Richard Tottel, 1559). Yale Elizabethan Club. Eliz. 157.
Anonymous manuscript copy, with some variations, of 1604. Yale Elizabethan Club. Eliz. 157A.
Toronto: Centre for Reformation and Renaissance Studies, Victoria University in the University of Toronto.
Raphael Holinshed, *The...Chronicles of England, Scotlande, and Irelande.* London: for John Hunne, 1577. (STC 13568b).DA 130 .H74 1557a.
Washington: Folger Shakespeare Library.
Ms. L.b.33. The Queen's warrant to the Master of the Revels for the loan of costumes.
Ms. L.b.109. List of costumes obtained from the Revels Office.

On microfilm

Richard Grafton, *An abridgement of the Chronicles of England, gathered by Richard Grafton, citizen of London, Anno Do. 1563.* London: Richard Tottel, 1563 (STC 12148), 165v-167v.

———. *Graftons abridgement of the chronicles of Englande. Newly and diligently corrected and finished the last of October 1570.* London: Richard Tottel, 1570 (STC 12151), 178v-179r.

———. *Graftons abridgement of the chronicles of Englande, newely corrected and augmented, to thys present yere of our Lord. 1572.* London: Richard Tottel, 1572 (STC 12152), 194r-195v.

Secondary Sources

Alford, Stephen. *The Early Elizabethan Polity: William Cecil and the British Succession Crisis, 1558-1569.* Cambridge: Cambridge University Press, 1998.

———. *Kingship and Politics in the Reign of Edward VI.* Cambridge: Cambridge University Press, 2002.

Allen, Thomas. *The history and antiquities of London, Westminster, Southwark and Parts Adjacent.* London: Jaques and Wright, 1827-1829.

Anglo, Sydney. *Spectacle, Pageantry, and Early Tudor Policy.* Oxford: Clarendon Press, 1969.

Archer, Ian. *The Pursuit of Stability: Social Relations in Elizabethan London.* Cambridge: Cambridge University Press. 1991.

Arnold, Janet. 'The 'Coronation' Portrait of Queen Elizabeth I.' *Burlington Magazine* 120 (November, 1978): 727-741 and plates.

———. *Queen Elizabeth's Wardrobe Unlock'd.* Leeds: Maney, 1988.

———. 'Jane Lambarde's Mantle.' *Costume* 14 (1980): 56-72.

Aston, Margaret. *The King's Bedpost: Reformation and Iconography in a Tudor Group Portrait.* Cambridge: Cambridge University Press, 1993.

Attreed, Lorraine. 'The Politics of Welcome: Ceremonies and Constitutional Development in Later Medieval English Towns.' In *City and Spectacle in*

Medieval Europe, edited by Barbara A. Hanawalt and Kathryn L. Reyerson, 208–231. Minneapolis: University of Minnesota Press, 1994.

Aylmer, John. *An harborowe for faithful and trewe subiects, agaynst the late blowne blast, concerning the government of wemen* [1559]. Facsimile edition. Amsterdam: Theatrum Orbis Terrarum, 1972.

Bartlett, Kenneth R. 'The Occasion of Lord Morley's Translation of the *Trionfi*.' In *Petrarch's Triumphs: Allegory and Spectacle*, edited by Konrad Eisenbichler and Amilcare A. Iannucci, 325–334. Ottawa: Dovehouse Editions, 1990.

Barker, William. 'Richard Mulcaster.' In *The Oxford Dictionary of National Biography* (forthcoming, 2004).

Baskervill, C.R. 'Richard Mulcaster.' *Times Literary Supplement* (August 15, 1935): 513.

Bayne, C.G. 'The Coronation of Queen Elizabeth.' *English Historical Review* 22 (1907): 650–673.

———. 'The Coronation of Queen Elizabeth.' [A different article by the same name.] *English Historical Review* 25 (1910): 550–553.

Bellorini, Mariagrazia. 'Da Londra a Mantova: Immagini di vita e di cultura inglese nella corrispondenza di Aloisio Schivenoglia (1556–1560).' *Studi di letteratura Inglese e Americana* (December, 1980): 57–92.

Bergeron, David. 'The Emblematic Nature of English Civic Pageantry.' *Renaissance Drama*. New Series 1 (1968): 167–198.

———. 'Symbolic Landscape in English Civic Pageantry.' *Renaissance Quarterly* 22.1 (1969): 32–37.

———. 'Venetian State Papers and English Civic Pageantry.' *Renaissance Quarterly* 23.1 (1970): 37–47.

———. *English Civic Pageantry, 1558–1642*. Columbia, SC: University of South Carolina Press, 1971.

———. 'Medieval Drama and Tudor-Stuart Pageantry.' *Journal of Medieval and Renaissance Studies* 2 (1972): 279–293.

———. 'Elizabeth's Coronation Entry (1559): New Manuscript Evidence.' *English Literary Renaissance* 8 (1978): 3–8 and plates.

Bertelli, Sergio. *The King's Body: Sacred Rituals of Power in Medieval and Early Modern Europe*. Trans. R. Burr Litchfield. University Park PA: The Pennsylvania State University Press, 2001.

Bochius, Johannes. *The Ceremonial Entry of Ernst, Archduke of Austria, into Antwerp, June 14, 1594*. Facsimile reprint with a new introduction by Hans Mielke. New York: Benjamin Blom, 1970.

Bowers, Roger. 'The Chapel Royal, The First Edwardian Prayer Book, and Elizabeth's Settlement of Religion, 1559,' *The Historical Journal* 43.2 (2000): 317–344.

Breitenberg, Mark. '"...the hole matter opened": Iconic Representation and Interpretation in "The Quenes Majesties Passage".' *Criticism* 28.1 (Winter, 1986): 1–25.

Bristol. Edited by Mark Pilkinton. Records of Early English Drama. Toronto: University of Toronto Press, 1997.

Bryant, Lawrence M. 'Configurations of the Community in Late Medieval Spectacles: Paris and London During the Dual Monarchy.' In *City and*

Spectacle in Medieval Europe. Edited by Barbara A. Hanawalt and Kathryn L. Reyerson, 3–33. Minneapolis: University of Minnesota Press, 1994.

Bucholz, R.O. *The Augustan Court: Queen Anne and the Decline of Court Culture.* Stanford: Stanford University Press, 1993.

Byrom, H.J. 'Richard Tottel – his Life and Work.' *The Library, Transactions of the Bibliographical Society.* Fourth Series 8 (1928): 199–232.

Camden, William. *The History of the Most Renowned and Victorious Princess Elizabeth, Late Queen of England.* Selected chapters edited by Wallace T. MacCaffrey. Chicago: University of Chicago Press, 1970.

Charity, Alan. *Events and their Afterlife: The Dialectics of Christian Typology in the Bible and Dante.* Cambridge: Cambridge University Press, 1966.

Collinson, Patrick. 'The Monarchical Republic of Queen Elizabeth I,' in *The Tudor Monarchy*, edited by John Guy, 110–134. London: Arnold, 1997.

Davis, Natalie Zemon. *The Gift in Sixteenth-Century France.* Madison: University of Wisconsin Press, 2000.

De Molen, Richard L. 'Richard Mulcaster and Elizabethan Pageantry.' *Studies in English Literature* 14 (1974): 209–221.

———. *Richard Mulcaster (c. 1531–1611) and Educational Reform in the Renaissance.* Nieuwkoop: De Graaf Publishers, 1991.

Duffy, Eamon. *The Stripping of the Altars: Traditional Religion in England, c. 1400–c. 1580.* New Haven: Yale University Press, 1992.

Edgerton William L. *Nicholas Udall.* New York: Twayne Publishers, 1965.

'E.H.' [Ellis, Sir Henry]. 'Biographical Anecdotes of Richard Mulcaster,' *Gentleman's Magazine* 70, part i (May 1800): 419–421, (June 1800): 511–512, part ii (July 1800): 602–604.

Elizabeth I. *The Collected Works of Elizabeth I.* Edited by Leah S. Marcus, Janel Mueller, and Mary Beth Rose. Chicago: University of Chicago Press, 2000.

Erasmus, Desiderius. *Julius Excluded from Heaven: A Dialogue.* Translated and annotated by Michael J. Heath. In *The Collected Works of Erasmus*, vol. 27. Edited by A.H.T. Levi. Toronto: University of Toronto Press, 1986.

Evelyn, John. *The Diary of John Evelyn.* Edited by E. S. de Beer. Oxford: Clarendon Press, 1955.

Fabyan, Robert. *The chronicle of Fabyan, whiche he hym selfe nameth the concordaunce of historyes.* London: [R. Grafton for] William Bonham or John Reynes, 1542.

———. *The Great Chronicle of London.* Edited by A.H. Thomas and I.D. Thornley (1938). Reprinted Gloucester: Alan Sutton, 1983.

Florio, John. *A Worlde of Wordes, or Most copious, and exact Dictionarie in Italian and English.* London: A. Hatfield for E. Blount, 1598.

Fosi, Irene. 'Court and City in the Ceremony of the *Possesso* in the Sixteenth Century.' In *Court and Politics in Papal Rome 1492–1700.* Edited by G. Signorotto and M.A. Visceglia, 31–52. Cambridge: Cambridge University Press, 2002.

Frye, Susan. *Elizabeth I: the Competition for Representation.* New York: Oxford University Press, 1993.

Geertz, Clifford. 'Centers, Kings and Charisma: Reflections on the Symbolics of Power.' In *Culture and its Creators: Essays in Honor of Edward Shils.*

Edited by Joseph Ben-David and Terry Nichols Clark, 150–171. Chicago: University of Chicago Press, 1977.

———. *Negara: the Theatre State in Nineteenth-Century Bali.* Princeton: Princeton University Press, 1980.

Gordon, Donald. 'Veritas filia temporis: Hadrianus Junius and Geoffrey Whitney.' *Journal of the Warburg and Courtauld Institutes* III (1939–1940): 228–240.

Gray, Douglas. 'The Royal Entry in Sixteenth-Century Scotland.' In *The Rose and the Thistle: Essays on the Culture of Late Medieval and Renaissance Scotland.* Edited by Sally Mapstone and Juliette Wood, 10–37. East Linton, East Lothian, Scotland: Tuckwell, 1998.

Hackett, Helen. *Virgin Mother, Maiden Queen.* London: Macmillan, 1995.

Haigh, Christopher. *Elizabeth I.* Second edition. London: Longman, 1998.

Haugaard, William P. 'The Coronation of Elizabeth I.' *Journal of Ecclesiastical History* 19.2 (October, 1968): 161–170.

Hayward, John. *Annals of the First Four Years of the Reign of Queen Elizabeth.* Edited by John Bruce, Camden Society no. 7. London, 1840.

Hazard, Mary. *Elizabethan Silent Language.* Lincoln, Nebraska: University of Nebraska Press, 2000.

Herbert, William. *The History of the Twelve Great Livery Companies of London.* Two volumes. London: published by the author, 1836–1837.

Heywood, Thomas. *If You Know Not Me, You Know No Bodie: or, The Troubles of Queene Elizabeth* (1605). Part I. Malone Society Reprints. London: Oxford University Press, 1934 [1935].

Hoak, Dale. 'The Iconography of the Crown Imperial.' In *Tudor Political Culture.* Edited by Dale Hoak, 54–103. Cambridge: Cambridge University Press, 1995.

———. 'A Tudor Deborah? The Coronation of Elizabeth I, Parliament, and the Problem of Female Rule.' In *John Foxe and his World.* Edited by Christopher Highley and John N. King, 73–88. Aldershot: Ashgate, 2002.

———. 'The Coronations of Edward VI, Mary I, and Elizabeth I, and the Transformation of the Tudor Monarchy.' In *Westminster Abbey Reformed 1540–1640.* Edited by C.S. Knighton and Richard Mortimer, 114–151. Aldershot: Ashgate, 2003.

Ingersoll, Richard. 'The Possesso, the Via Papale, and the Stigma of Pope Joan' In *Urban Rituals in Italy and the Netherlands: Historical Contrasts in the Use of Public Space.* Edited by Heidi De Mare and Anna Vos, 39–50. Assen: Van Gorcum, 1993.

Inglis, Erik. 'A Book in the Hand: Some Late Medieval Accounts of Manuscript Presentations.' *Journal of the Early Book Society* 5 (2002): 57–97, 70.

Ives, E.W. *Anne Boleyn.* Oxford: Basil Blackwell, 1986.

Johns, Adrian. *The Nature of the Book: Print and Knowledge in the Making.* University of Chicago Press, 1998.

Johnston, Alexandra F. 'English Civic Ceremony' in *Petrarch's Triumphs: Allegory and Spectacle.* Edited by Konrad Eisenbichler and Amilcare A. Iannucci, 395–402. Ottawa: Dovehouse Editions, 1990.

Kantorowicz, Ernst H. 'The "King's Advent" and the Enigmatic Panels in the Doors of Santa Sabina.' In his *Selected Studies*, 37–75. Locust Valley NY: J.J.Augustin, 1965.

Katzenellenbogen, Adolph. *Allegories of the Virtues and Vices in Medieval Art from Early Christian Times to the Thirteenth Century*. New York: W.W. Norton, 1964.

King, John N. *Tudor Royal Iconography: Literature and Art in an Age of Religious Crisis*. Princeton: Princeton University Press, 1989.

———. 'The royal image, 1535–1603.' in *Tudor Political Culture*. Edited by Dale Hoak, 104–132. Cambridge: Cambridge University Press, 1995.

Kingdon, John Abernethy. *Richard Grafton, Citizen and Grocer of London*. London, privately printed, 1901.

Kinser, Samuel. 'Presentation and Representation: Carnival at Nuremberg, 1450–1550.' *Representations* 13 (Winter, 1986): 1–42.

Kinney, Arthur, ed. 'The Queen's Majesty's Passage,' in *Renaissance Drama: An Anthology of Plays and Entertainments*. Malden, Mass.: Blackwell, 1999.

Kipling, Gordon. 'Triumphal Drama: Form in English Civic Pageantry.' *Renaissance Drama*, New Series 8 (1977): 49–50.

———. *Enter the King: Theatre, Liturgy and Ritual in the Medieval Civic Triumph*. Oxford: Clarendon Press, 1998.

Kipling, Gordon, ed. *The receyt of the ladie Kateryne*, EETS no. 296. Oxford: Early English Text Society, 1990.

Knoppers, Laura L. *Constructing Cromwell: Ceremony, Portrait, and Print 1645–1661*. Cambridge: Cambridge University Press, 2000.

Knox, John. *The First Blast of the Trumpet Against the Monstrous Regiment of Women*. Facsimile of 1558 edition. Amsterdam: Theatrum orbis terrarum, 1972.

———. *The Works of John Knox*. Ed. David Laing. Edinburgh: Thomas George Stevenson, 1854–1864.

Lancashire, Anne K. 'Continuing Civic Ceremonies of 1530s London.' In *Civic Ritual and Drama*. Edited by Alexandra F. Johnston and Wim Hüsken, 81–105. Amsterdam: Editions Rodopi, 1997.

Lancashire, Ian. *Dramatic Texts and Records of Britain: A Chronological Topography to 1558*. Toronto: University of Toronto Press, 1984.

Leahy, William. 'Propaganda or a Record of Events? Richard Mulcaster's *The Passage of Our Most Drad Soveraine Lady Quene Elyzabeth Through the Citie of London Westminster the Daye Before Her Coronacion*,' *Early Modern Literary Studies* 9.1 (May, 2003): 3.1–20. <http://purl.oclc.org/emls/09-1/leahmulc.html>

Legg, Leopold G. Wickham, ed. *English Coronation Records*. Westminster: Archibald Constable, 1901.

Lindenbaum, Sheila. 'Ceremony and Oligarchy: The London Midsummer Watch.' in *City and Spectacle in Medieval Europe*. Edited by Barbara A. Hanawalt and Kathryn L. Reyerson, 171–188. Minneapolis: University of Minnesota Press, 1994.

Loades, David. *The Reign of Mary Tudor: Politics, Government and Religion in England, 1553–1558*. Second edition. London: Longman 1991.

Logan, Sandra. 'Making History: The Rhetorical and Historical Occasion of Elizabeth Tudor's Coronation Entry,' *Journal of Medieval and Early Modern Literary Studies* 31.2 (Spring, 2001): 251–282.

Luzio, Alessandro. 'I carteggi dell'Archivio Gonzaga riflettenti l'Inghilterra.' *Atti delle R. Accademia dell scienze di Torino* 23 (1917–1918): 25–40.

MacCaffrey, Wallace. *Elizabeth I*. London: Edward Arnold, 1993.

MacCormack, Sabine. *Art and Ceremony in Late Antiquity*. Berkeley: University of California Press, 1981.

MacCulloch, Diarmaid. *Tudor Church Militant: Edward VI and the Protestant Reformation*. London: Allen Lane, 1999

Machyn, Henry. *The Diary of Henry Machyn, Citizen and Merchant-Taylor of London, from A.D. 1550 to A.D. 1563*. Edited by John Gough Nichols. Camden Society no. 42. London, 1848.

Maclean, Ian. *The Renaissance Notion of Woman: A Study in the Fortunes of Scholasticism and Medical Science in European Intellectual Life*. Cambridge: Cambridge University Press, 1980.

Manning, John. 'Emblems.' In *The Spenser Encyclopedia*, 247–249. Edited by A.C. Hamilton et al., Toronto: University of Toronto Press, 1990.

Mauss, Marcel. *The Gift: the Form and Reason for Exchange in Archaic Societies* [1925]. Trans. W. D. Halls. London: Routledge, 1990.

McCoy, Richard C. '"Thou Idol Ceremony": Elizabeth I, *The Henriad*, and the Rites of the English Monarchy,' in *Urban Life in the Renaissance*. Edited by Susan Zimmerman and Ronald F.C. Weissman, 240–260. Newark NJ: University of Delaware Press, 1989.

McLaren, A.N. *Political Culture in the Reign of Elizabeth I: Queen and Commonwealth 1558–1585*. Cambridge: Cambridge University Press, 1999.

McCormick, Michael. *Eternal Victory: Triumphal Rulership in Late Antiquity, Byzantium and the Early Medieval West*. Cambridge: Cambridge University Press, 1986.

Mercurius Politicus, no. 191, in *The English Revolution*, III, Newsbooks 5, Volume 8, *Mercurius Politicus 1653–1654*. London: Cornmarket Press, 1971– .

McCracken, Grant. 'The Pre-Coronation Passage of Elizabeth I: Political Theatre or the Rehearsal of Politics?' *Canadian Review of Sociology and Anthropology* 21.1 (1984): 47–61.

Mitchell, Bonner. *Italian Civic Pageantry in the High Renaissance: A Descriptive Bibliography of Triumphal Entries and Selected Other Festivals for State Occasions*. Firenze: Leo S. Olschki Editore, 1979.

Montrose, Louis Adrian. 'Gifts and Reasons: The Contexts of Peele's Araygnment of Paris.' *English Literary Renaissance* 47 (1980): 433–461.

Muir, Edward. *Ritual in Early Modern Europe*. Cambridge: Cambridge University Press, 1997.

Mulcaster, Richard. *Positions Concerning the Training up of Children*. Ed. William Barker. Toronto: University of Toronto Press, 1994.

———. *The first part of the elementarie*. London: 1582.

Mullaney, Stephen. *The Place of the Stage: License, Play and Power in Renaissance England*. Chicago: University of Chicago Press, 1988.

Neale, J.E. *Queen Elizabeth*. London: Jonathan Cape, 1934.

Nichols, John, ed. *The Progresses and Public Processions of Queen Elizabeth.* 3 volumes. London: John Nichols and Son, 1823.

Nichols, John Gough, ed. *The Chronicle of Queen Jane and of Two Years of Queen Mary.* Camden Society no. 48. London, 1850.

———. *Literary Remains of King Edward the Sixth* [1857]. Reprinted New York: Burt Franklin, 1963.

Osborn, James M., ed. *The Quenes Maiesties Passage through the Citie of London to Westminster the Day before her Coronacion.* Introduction by Sir John Neale. Published for the Elizabethan Club. New Haven: Yale University Press, 1960.

Parry, Graham. *The Golden Age Restor'd: The Culture of the Stuart Court 1603–1642.* Manchester: Manchester University Press, 1981.

Parsons, John Carmi. 'Ritual and Symbol in the English Medieval Queenship to 1500.' In *Women and Sovereignty.* Edited by Louise Olga Fradenburg, 60–77. Edinburgh: Edinburgh University Press, 1992.

———. 'The Pregnant Queen as Counsellor and the Medieval Construction of Motherhood.' In *Medieval Mothering*, ed. John Carmi Parsons and Bonnie Wheeler, 39–61. New York: Garland, 1996.

Perrott, Sir James. *The history of that eminent statesman, Sir John Perrott, Knight of the Bath, and Lord Lieutenant of Ireland.* Edited by Richard Rawlinson. London, 1728.

Phythian-Adams, Charles. 'Ceremony and the Citizen: The Communal Year at Coventry 1450–1550.' In *Crisis and Order in English Towns 1500–1700: Essays in Urban History.* Edited by Peter Clark and Paul Slack, 57–85. London: Routledge and Kegan Paul, 1972.

Pingree, David, ed. *Picatrix. The Latin Version of the Ghyat-al-hakm.* Studies of the Warburg Institute, v. 39. London: The Warburg Institute, 1986.

Plattus, Alan. 'Emblems of the City: Civic Pageantry and the Rhetoric of Urbanism.' *Artforum* 20.1 (September, 1981): 48–52.

Pollard, A.F., ed. *Tudor Tracts 1532–1588.* Westminster: Constable, 1903.

Prockter, Adrian and Robert Taylor, eds. *The A to Z of Elizabethan London*, publication no. 122. London: London Topographical Society, 1979.

Judith M. Richards. '"His Nowe Majestie" and the English Monarchy: The Kingship of Charles I Before 1640.' *Past and Present* 113 (1986): 70–96.

———. 'Mary Tudor as "Sole Quene"? Gendering Tudor Monarchy.' *The Historical Journal* 404 (1997): 895–924.

———. '"To Promote a Woman to Beare Rule": Talking of Queens in Mid-Tudor England.' *Sixteenth Century Journal* 28.1 (1997): 101–121.

———. 'Love and a Female Monarch: The Case of Elizabeth Tudor.' *Journal of British Studies* 38 (April 1999): 133–160.

Robertson, Jean. 'L'entrée de Charles quint à Londres, en 1522,' in *Les Fêtes de la Renaissance*, edited by Jean Jacquot, I, 169–181. Two volumes. Paris: Éditions du centre national de la recherche scientifique. 1956, 1960.

Robertson, Jean, and D.J. Gordon, eds. 'A Calendar of Dramatic Records in the Books of the Livery Companies of London 1485-1640.' In *Collections* III, Malone Society: xiii–xlvi. Oxford: Oxford University Press, 1954.

Bibliography 151

Rodriguez-Salgado, M.J., and Simon Adams, ed. and trans. 'The Count of Feria's Dispatch to Philip II of 14 November 1558.' In *Camden Miscellany* 28: 302-44. London: Royal Historical Society, 1984.

Rykwert, Joseph. *The Idea of a Town: the Anthropology of Urban Form in Rome, Italy and the Ancient World*. Revised edition, Cambridge MA: The MIT Press, 1988.

Saxl, Fritz. 'Veritas filia temporis.' in *Philosophy and History: Essays Presented to Ernst Cassirer*. Edited by Raymond Klibansky and H.J. Paton, 197–222. Oxford: Clarendon Press, 1936.

Schofield, John, ed. *The London Surveys of Ralph Treswell*. London Topographical Society, Publication no. 135, 1987.

Schramm, Percy E. *A History of the English Coronation*. Trans. Leopold G. Wickham Legge. Oxford: Clarendon Press, 1937.

Schwerer, Lois. 'The Glorious Revolution as Spectacle: A New Perspective.' In *England's Rise to Greatness 1660–1763*. Edited by Stephen B. Baxter, 109–149. Berkeley: University of California Press, 1983.

Scribner, Bob. 'Cosmic Order and Daily Life: Sacred and Secular in Pre-Industrial German Society.' In *Religion and Society in Early Modern Europe 1500–1800*. Edited by Kaspar von Greyertz, 17–32. London: George Allen and Unwin, 1984.

Sherman, William H. *John Dee: The Politics of Reading and Writing in the English Renaissance*. Amherst, Mass.: University of Massachusetts Press, 1995

Sherwood, Roy. *The Court of Oliver Cromwell*. London: Croom Helm, 1977.

Shils, Edward. 'Charisma, Order and Status.' *American Sociological Review* 30 (1965): 199–213.

Sisson, C.J. 'Grafton and the London Grey Friars,' *The Library*, Fourth Series, 11.2 (September 1930), 121–149.

Smith, E. Baldwin. *Architectural Symbolism of Imperial Rome and the Middle Ages*. Princeton, N.J.: Princeton University Press, 1956.

Smuts, R. Malcolm. 'Public Ceremony and Royal Charisma: the English Royal Entry in London, 1485–1642.' In *The First Modern Society: Essays in English History in Honour of Lawrence Stone*. Edited by A.L. Beier, David Cannadine, and James M. Rosenheim, 65–93. Cambridge: Cambridge University Press, 1989.

Stow, John. *The Annales, or Generall Chronicle of England...continued unto ...1614 by E. Howes*. London: 1615.

———. *A Survey of London*. Edited by C.L. Kingsford, 2 vols. Oxford: Clarendon Press, 1908.

Streitberger, W.R. *Court Revels, 1485–1559*. Toronto: University of Toronto Press, 1994.

Strong, Roy C. 'Elizabethan Pageantry as Propaganda.' PhD diss., University of London, 1962.

———. *Art and Power: Renaissance Festivals 1450–1650*. Woodbridge, UK: Boydell Press, 1984.

———. *The Tudor and Stuart Monarchy: Pageantry, Painting, Iconography*. 3 vols. Woodbridge, UK: Boydell Press, 1995.

———, and J.A. Van Dorsten. *Leicester's Triumph*. Leiden: Leiden University Press for the Sir Thomas Browne Institute,1964.
Strype, John. *Annals of the Reformation and Establishment of Religion*. Oxford: Clarendon Press, 1824.
Turner, Victor. *The Ritual Process: Structure and Anti-structure*. London: Routledge & Kegan Paul, 1969.
Van Gennep, Arnold. *The rites of passage*. Trans. Monika B. Vizedom and Gabrielle L. Caffee. Chicago: University of Chicago Press, 1960.
Von Klarwill,Victor, ed. *Queen Elizabeth and Some Foreigners*. Trans. T.H. Nash. London: John Lane The Bodley Head, 1928.
Wagner, Marie-France and Daniel Vaillancourt, eds., *Le Roi dans la ville: Anthologie des entrées royales dans les villes françaises de province (1615–1660)*. Paris: Honoré Champion, 2001.
Wall, Wendy. *The Imprint of Gender: Authorship and Publication in the English Renaissance*. Ithaca: Cornell University Press, 1993.
Ward, Joseph P. *Metropolitan Communities: Trade Guilds, Identity, and Change in Early Modern London*. Stanford: Stanford University Press, 1997.
Watkins, John. '"Old Bess in the Ruff": Remembering Elizabeth I, 1625–1660.' *English Literary Renaissance* 30.1 (Winter, 2000), 95–116.
Weber, Max. *On Charisma and Institution Building: Selected Papers*, ed. S.N. Eisenstadt. Chicago: University of Chicago Press, 1968.
Weinreb, Ben, and Christopher Hibbert, eds. *The London Encyclopedia*. Second edition, revised. London: Macmillan, 1993.
Westrem, Scott. 'Against Gog and Magog.' In *Text and Territory: Geographical Imagination in the European Middle Ages*. Edited by Sylvia Tomasch and Sealy Gilles, 34–75. Philadelphia: University of Pennsylvania Press, 1998.
Wilson, Arthur. *The History of Great Britain, being The Life and Reign of King James the First*. London, 1653.
Wilson, Jean. *Entertainments for Elizabeth*. Woodbridge, UK: Boydell and Brewer, 1980.
Withington, Robert. 'The Early "Royal-Entry"' *PMLA* 32 (December, 1917), 616–623.
———. *English Pageantry*. 2 vols, Cambridge: Harvard University Press, 1918–1920.
Woolf, D.R. 'The Power of the Past: History, Ritual and Political Authority in Tudor England.' In *Political Thought and the Tudor Commonwealth: Deep Structure, Discourse and Disguise*, edited by Paul A. Fideler and T.F. Mayer, 19–49. London: Routledge, 1992.
Wriothesley, Charles. *A Chronicle of England During the Reigns of the Tudors, from AD 1485 to 1559*. Ed. W. D. Hamilton. London: Camden Society new series, vols. 11, 20, 1875–1877.
Yates, Frances. *Astraea: the Imperial Theme in the Sixteenth Century*. London: Routledge and Kegan Paul, 1975.
York. Edited by Alexandra F. Johnston and Margaret Rogerson. 2 volumes. Records of Early English Drama. Toronto: University of Toronto Press, 1979.

Index

The index covers proper names, place names, basic themes and concepts mentioned in the Introduction, the text of the entry, Appendices I and II, and the Textual Note. Any substantive references in the footnotes are also included. Since Elizabeth I herself is mentioned on almost every page of the volume, index references to her have been kept to essentials.

Acts of Uniformity and of Supremacy, 30
adventus, see triumph, royal entry, Papal *possesso*
Alford, Stephen, 15, 66
Allen, George, 118
Allen, Thomas, 139
'Allegory of the Tudor Succession,' fig. 3
Altham, Master, 116
Andrewes, Lancelot, 16
Anglo, Sydney, 54
Arnold, Janet, 33
Arundel, see Fitzalan
Ascham, Roger, 29
Astraea, *see* Elizabeth I
Atkinson, Giles, 119
Aurifex, *see* Goldsmith
Aylmer, John, 66–67, 73
Bannister, Thomas, 117, 120
Barbican, 44, 101
Barges, 99, 104
Barker, Francis, 118
Barnes, Richard, 118
Barnet town, 101; *and see* Middlesex, 116
Barnham, Francis, 118
Baskervill, C.R., 16n5
Beacher, Henry, 120
beating the bounds, *see* lustration
Beatitudes, pageant of, 40, 57, 83–85, 112
Becket, Thomas, 102 *and* n11
'Beningfield,' 73
Bergeron, David, see footnotes, 122–23
bible: 'the Bible in English,' 37, 55, 58, 59, fig. 12, 63, 86, 98, 112; *see also* typology

Bishopsgate, 44, 101
Blackfriars, 104
Boleyn, Anne (queen), 26, 28, 35, 41, 45, 52, 57, 78, 100, 107; as 'saving Hester,' 67
Book of Common Prayer, 30
Braun and Haugenberg map (1572), 48–49, fig. 10
Broskerby, Bartholomew, 119
Browne, Richard, 119
Browne, Thomas, 118
Bucholz, R.O., 71
Buckfold, Henry, 118
Buckland, Richard, 118, 121
Busby, John, 141
Caius, John, 40
Calais, 75n2, 110
Calandra, Sabino, Castellan of Mantua, 16, 103, 140, 142
Calvin, John, 66n132
Camden, William, 15
Carew, George, 70
Carpenters' Company, member of, 118
Castell, Thomas, 118
Cawarden, Sir Thomas, Master of the Revels, 45, fig. 8, 121–22
Cecil, William (later Lord Burghley), 15, 26, 31, 35, 37, 58, 70; memorandum on the accession, 35n68
Chancellors, 105; *and see* Great Seal, Privy Seal
Chapel Royal, 100
Charles I (king), 71
Charles II (king), 71
Charles V (emperor), 26, 102
Charterhouse, 44, 101, 111
Chaucer, Geoffrey, 25

Cheapside, 37, 49 *and* n98, 96, 97, 108, 121; Cheapside Cross, 25, 49 *and* n99, fig. 11, 59, 85, 108, 118, 120
Cheke, John, 29
Chelsham, William, 120
Chester, 25
Chief Butler, 120 *and* n14
Cholmely, Ranulph, Recorder of London, 61, 86, 97, 100, 108
Christ's Hospital, children of, fig. 5b, 68, 93, 97, 109, 121, 124; *see also* Hospitals, Royal
Chyvall, William, 120
circuitus murorum, *see* lustration
Clothworkers' Company, members of, 118
Colet, John, 49, 90
conduits, *see* Little Conduit, Great Conduit, Fleet, Cornhill
Corineus, *see* Gotmagot and Corineus
Cornhill, 37, 54, 57, 81, 96, 100, 107, 111; Conduit in Cornhill, 107, 117
Cornwall, Clement, 118
coronation: customs and rituals, 15, 26–28, and see *Forma et modus*; coronation rite today, 72; Machyn's description, 100; religious ceremony, 69; state banquet, 27, 72
'Coronation portrait,' cover, 3
Cottonian Library, 100
Court of Aldermen, see London
Court, Royal, 16, 19, 35, 58, 59, 69, 71, 103–106, 115; *see also* Lord Chamberlain *and* Master of the Revels
Coventry, 25
Cranmer, Thomas, archbishop of Canterbury, 28
Craythorne, John, 118
Cripplegate, 44, 101
Cromwell, Oliver, 71
'crown imperial,' 29, 57, 65, 78 *and* n18, 82, 91n60
Cupboard, attending at, 120 *and* n13
Cutlers' Company, members of, 118
Dame, William, 120
Daniel, 68, 98, 111
David (king of Israel), 24, 67

Deborah, 33, 58, 67, 73; *Deborah the judge and restorer of the house of Israel*, pageant of, 40, 55, 65–68, 73, 91–93, 109, 112
Dee, John, 26
Dekker, Thomas, 23, 71
Doge of Venice, 21, 103 *and* n14
Douglas, Lady Margaret, countess of Lennox, 31
Drapers' Company, members of, 118, 120
Ducket, Lionel, 37, 46, 119
Dudley, John, duke of Northumberland, 28
Dudley, Robert, later earl of Leicester, 44 *and* n87, 106, 110
Dutch pageants for James I, 52
Eagle, sign of, 78
Edward the Confessor (king), 69
Edward IV (king), 78, 79, 112
Edward VI (king), 24, 26, 28, 30, 40, fig. 11, 59, 63, 67, 69, 93. 100, 111
Eleanor Cross, *see* Cheapside Cross
Elizabeth I, Queen (see headnote): as Astraea, 65, 73; as Gloriana 74; background, gender, political and religious situation, 28–33; chastity, 32–33, 70, 74; coronation entry into London, 15 and *passim*, 75–98, *and see* frontispiece; coronation portrait, cover, 3, 33, 115; enters Saffron Walden (1571) and Norwich (1578), 70; other entries into London, 70; garb and hair on the day of the entry, 33, 123–24; imprisonment in the Tower, 43, 45, 98; pageant figure wearing imperial crown, 57; prayer on leaving the Tower, 98; preparating for the entry 43–45; progresses and entertainments, 55; reads typologically, 68; responsiveness and spontaneity, 53, 56, 58, 61, 77, 85, 97; 'Time hath brought me hither,' 59, 85
Elizabeth of York (queen), 57, 78–80, 107, 112
Elizabethan Settlement, *see* Act of Uniformity and Act of Supremacy
Elliot, John, 121–23

Index 155

Elrington, Edward, 120n14
Erasmus, Desiderius, 22
Evelyn, John, 71
Fabyan, Robert, 40 *and* n73, 74
Faerie Queene, The, 65, 74
farewell, *see* Temple Bar
Fenchurch Street, 37, 44, 86, 118; welcome at, 55–56, 76–77, 103
Feria, see Suarez de Figueroa
Ferrer, Richard, 118
Fishmongers' Company, member of, 120
Fitzalan, Henry, earl of Arundel, 105, 120n14
Fleet bridge, 48, 91, 97; Fleet Street, 49, 109, 111, 121; conduit in, 57, 65, 73, 91, 100, 118
Fleet prison, Farringdon Street, 63
Florentine pageants for entry of Mary I, 52
Forma et modus, 27 *and* n38
Fortunatus, Venantius, 100
Founders' Company, members of, 118
Foxe, John, 28
Fyshe, Walter (queen's tailor), 33, fig. 4, 115, 123–24
gates, city, 20, *and* n10, 72; St. Peter's gates 22; *see also* Cripplegate, Bishopsgate, Ludgate
Geertz, Clifford, 21
Gentleman Pensioners, 106
George II (king), 32n59, 72
Gibbons, William, 120
Gifts, 23, 53, 54–56, 58, 68, 76–77; the City's gift to the queen, 46, 61, 86, 95, 100, 108, 113, 116–17; *see also* Bible
Girdlers' Company, members of, 118
'Gog and Magog', *see* Gotmagot and Corineus
Goldsmiths' Company, members of (Aurifex), 118, 120
Gotmagot and Corineus ('Gog and Magog'), 33 *and* n64, fig. 5a, 54, 68, 93, 100, 109
Grace, Richard, 118
Gracechurch Street, 44, 54, 56, 63, 78, 100, 107, 111
Gracious Street, *see* Gracechurch Street.

Grafton Richard: appointed to supervise preparations, 37, 46, 119; background, 26, 37, 40; death, 74; friendship with Nicholas Udall, 41; *Chronicle* versions of the entry, 110–13; involvement in 1554 entry, 63, 65; Warden of Christ's Hospital, 68; writings, 52; mentioned, 16, 19, 35, 54, 56, 58, 59, 69, 103
Great Conduit in Cheap, 25, 37, 49, 54, 57, 83, 107, 118, 120–21
Great Seal, 105
Gresham, John, 121–22
Grey, Lady Catherine, 31
Grey, Lady Jane ('Queen Jane'), 28, 30, 31, 37, 67
Grocers' Company, 26, 37, 40, 46, 74; members of, 118–20
Gunter, Philip, 117
Gylberd, Edward, 118
Haberdashers' Company, members of, 118, 120, 121
Habsburg empire, 29
Hackett, Helen, 72
Hall, Edward, 37, 110
Hamilton, W.D., 101
Hanseatic pageants for entry of Mary I, 52
Harrison, John, 118, 120
Harrison, William, 99
Hatfield Palace, 44, 75, 101, 111
Hayward, John, 43
Hayward, Roland, 118, 120
Heaton, George, 118
Henry III (king), 48
Henry V (king), 40
Henry VI (king), 40
Henry VII (king), 24, 57, 67, 70, 78–80, 102, 107, 112
Henry VIII (king), 28, 29, fig. 3, 31, 35, 59, 63, 66, 78–80, 93, 97, 100, 107, 111
Heralds, 35, 105; Garter King of Arms, 44, 105; Windsor Herald, 16, 101
Herbert, William, earl of Pembroke, 44
Hester, 67 *and* n137
Heywood, Thomas, 73; *If You Know Not Me, You Know No Body*, 73–74

Hilles, Richard, 37, 40n75, 46, 119
Holinshed, Raphael, 44, 73, 74, 99, 139
Hospitals, Royal, 26, *and see* Christ's Hospital
Howard, Thomas, Duke of Norfolk, 105
Hulson, John, 118
Hunne, John, 99, 141
Hunt, Thomas, 117
Ironmongers' Company, members of, 118, 120
Italian pageants for entry of James I, 52, 58n11
Jackson, John, 118
James I (king), 16, 23, 24, 58n11, 70–71
James, William, 119
Jesse, *see* Tree of Jesse
Jesus, entry into Jerusalem, 20
Johnston, Alexandra F., 71
Jonson, Ben, 71
Jorden, William (queen's skinner), 123
Julius II (pope), 22
Julius exclusus, 22
Katherine of Aragon (queen), 28, 53, 56, 72
King, John N., 63
Kinney, Arthur, 139
Kipling, Gordon, 20n12, 53
Knights of the Bath, 27, 52 *and* n100, 103, 104
Knox, John, 63, 66 *and* n132, 67
Kyd, Thomas, 16
Lacy, John, 118
Leadenhall, 44
Lee, Edward, 120
Lee, Garrard, 118
Legg, Leopold G. Wickham, 27n38
Leicester, earl of, see Dudley
Leigh, Thomas, Mercer, Lord Mayor of London, 121n18, *and see* London
Leland, John, 41
Lennox, see Douglas
Liber regalis, 27n38
Little Conduit in Cheap, 22, 24, 37, 49, 55, 58, 59, 61, 85, 86, 87, 98, 100, 103, 108, 111, 118
Little Device, 27n38
Liturgy: English, 29–30, 102; Latin, 30; at coronation, 69–70
Livery Companies, 'Twelve Great,' 47n92, *and see names of companies*

Lodge, Thomas, 16
Lollards, 25
London Bridge, 101, 104
London: Aldermen plan the entry, 115–25, *passim*; Chamberlain, 100, 124–25; City as ritual space, 48–52; Civic barge, 99; Common Council, 35, 46, 48; Court of Aldermen, 16, 35, 37, 41, 46–48; Lord Mayor, 25 *and* n31, 26, 35, 86, 105, 111, 113, 121n18; Master Sheriffs, 46, 101, 116; Southwark, 25
London Wall, 44, 101
Lord Chamberlain, 106, 115
Lowe, Thomas, 120
Ludgate, 37, 49, 113, 118; prisoners in, 68, 91n57, 109; noise of instruments at, 91
lustration, 45 *and* n89.
Lydgate, John, 40
Machyn, Henry, 16, 25, 99–100
Malory, Master 116
Marian martyrs, 28
Mark Lane, 44, 55 *and* n108
Marston, Thomas, 118
Marten, Master, 116
Mary I (queen), 15, 26, 28–30, fig. 3, 33, 37, 40, 43, 45, 48, 52, 59, 63, 69, 101–02, 103, 110, 111, 115, 117, 123
Mary II (queen), 71
Mary (Queen of Scots), 31, 66
Master of the Revels, 45, fig. 8, 115, 121–22
Medici family, 21
Mercers' Company, 37, 46; bachelors of, 99, 121; chapel, 102; members of, 118–20
Merchant Taylors' Company, 46; school, 16; members of, 117–19
Midsummer Watch, 25, 35
Mielke, Hans, 21
Millington, Jone [Joan], 141
Misrule, Lord of, 25
Mordyng, Myles, 117
Mortimer, William, 118
Mulcaster, Richard: birth and background, 16, 40–43; *Elementarie*, 23, 43, 74; influence of his account of the procession

Index 157

74; later career, 74; paid for 'making the book,' 41, fig. 7, 124–25; *Positions*, 41, 43, 74; mentioned or quoted, 52, 54, 55, 56, 58, 61, 63, 65, 69, 70, 103
Mullaney, Steven, 70
Music, minstrels, waits, 56, 76, 79, 81, 82, 84, 85, 91, 95, 116; 'Salve festa dies,' 100
Nayler, Henry, 118
Nestor, 90
Nicholl, Thomas, 118
Nichols, John, 70, 74, 139
Nine worthies, pageant of, 1554, 63
Norfolk, duke of, see Howard
North, Sir Edward, 44 *and* n86, 101, 111
Northumberland, duke of, see Dudley, John
Offley, Robert, 118
Oglethorpe, Owen, bishop of Carlisle, 70
Osborn, James, 141
Otto, emperor, 25
pageants, 22 *and* n21; defined, 135; pageant-making as a profession, 41–43, 71, 103
Painters and Stainers Company, 25, 120 *and* n15, 121
Papal *possesso*, 21
Parliament, 31, 102
Parr, Catherine (queen), 29
Parrat (or Perrot), Sir John, 59 *and* n119, 61, 63, 86, 142
Pearson, Thomas, 118
Pembroke, earl of, see Herbert
Percy, General Lord Henry H.M., 101
Perkyn Revelour, 25, 49
Peterson, William, 118
Petrarca, Francesco (Petrarch), 22
Philip II (king of Spain), 26, 29, 40, 44, 63, 101
Plato, *Republic*, 65, 89
Playne, David, 120–21
Pole, Reginald, cardinal, 101
Printing, publication and influence of the pamphlet, 16–19, 72–74, *and see* Textual Note.
Privy Council, 15, 31, 35, 69, 102, 105
Privy Seal, 105

processions, civic, 24–26
Protectorate, 71
Prudentius, *Psychomachia*, 57 *and* n111
Pycket, Thomas, 118
queen consort *and* queen regnant, 32
Revelour, Perkyn, see Perkyn
'ribald' figure, 20
Richard III (king), 24
Richards, Judith M., 31
Ridley, Nicholas, bishop of Lincoln, 28
rites of passage, 27
Robinson, Francis, 37, 46, 119, 120
Rowe, Master, 116
royal entry, 19–28, and *passim*; design of, 52–58; English entries, 21n15; entry as process, 53; as a means of counsel and instruction, 20, 56–58
Ruinosa respublica and *Respublica bene instituta*, pageant of, see *Time and Truth*, pageant of
St. Dunstan's in the West, 93, 121
St. James, manor of, at Charing Cross, 101
St. Mary-le-Bow, 49
St. Matthew, Gospel of, 57, 84, 108
St. Michael le Querne, 61, fig.13
St. Paul's Cathedral, 24, 49, 73, 104, 109; churchyard, 73, 88, 89, 109.
St. Paul's School, 16, 49, 65, 73, 89–91, 109, 140
St. Peter's Church, 85
St. Thomas's Church, 108
Salters' Company, member of, 120
San Giorgio, Castle of, 103
Schivenoglia, Aloisio, "Il Schifanoia", 16, 52, 58, 68; narrative of the entry, 103–10, 139–41
Scriveners' Company, members of, 118–19
Seals, see Great Seal *and* Privy Seal
Seat of Worthy Governance, pageant of, 57, 58, 81–83, 112
Seymour, Edward, duke of Somerset, 28
Sheppard, John, 100n5
Skinners' Company, members of, 117–18, 120
Smithfield Market, 44; East Smithfield, 48

Smuts, R. Malcolm, 19
Somerset, duke of, see Seymour
Somerset House, 45, 101
Soper's Lane, 57, 83, 100, 111
Spenser, Edmund, 16, 65, 74
Sponer, Thomas, 118
Stafford, Simon, 141
Standard, the, 24, 37, 49, 85, 108, 118
Stationers' Company, member of, 119
Stockbridge, Richard, 118
Stocks, 117
Stow, John, 28, 70
Strand, 71
Strong, Roy C., 16n5, 19, 20
Strype, John, 35n68, 43, 45, 74, 139
Suarez de Figueroa, Gomez, count of Feria, 44 *and* n85, 66, 105
succession to the crown, 30–31, fig. 3
Taylor, Laurence, 118
Taylor, Richard, 118
Temple Bar, 15, 16, 27, 37, 49, 55, 56, 68, 69, 93, 95, 98; farewell at Temple Bar, 56, 68, 93–95, 100, 119
Temporis filia (Truth or *Veritas,* the daughter of Time), 62, 87; *see also* '*Veritas temporis filia*'
Throckmorton, Sir Nicholas, 35n68
Time and Truth: emblematic image of, title page, 3, 63, fig. 14, 57, 58; pageant of, 40, 59, 87–89, 108, 112; see also '*Veritas temporis filia*'
Tottel, Richard, 16, 98, 110, 119, 139, 141
Tower of London, 15, 25, 27, 44, 48, 49, 52, 75, 76, 86, 99, 100, 101, 102, 103, 104, 111; Elizabeth's imprisonment in, 43, 45, 98; Tower Hill, 45, 106; Tower Street, 44
Traves, John, 117
Tree of Jesse, 78n17
Tresham, Sir Thomas, 103
Treswell, Ralph, fig. 13

Trionfi (Petrarch), 22
Triumph (*adventus*), 20, *and* n11, 23, 71, 72, *and see* royal entry
typology, 24 *and* n28, 67–8
Udall, Nicholas, 41 *and* n79
Uniting of the two houses of Lancaster and York, pageant of, 56–57, 78–81, 112
Venice, Ascension Day, 103
Verbum dei, 63
Veritas temporis filia (Truth, the daughter of Time), 3, 62–63, fig. 14
Vintner's Company, member of, 120; Vintry, 99
Wades, Robert, 120
Walkeden, Geoffrey, 118
Wardrobe, 106, 124
Watkins, John, 74
Weber, Max, 43
Wedel, Lupold von, 70
welcome, *see* Fenchurch Street
Westminster, 25, 58, 68; 75, 95, 97, 124; Abbey, 15, 27, 45, 69, 100, 101, 102; abbot of, 105; Hall, 100, 102
Whitchurch, Edward, 37
Whitehall Palace, 45, 102, 103, 110
Whittingham, William, 63, fig. 14
William III (king), 71
Wilson, Arthur, 71
Wilson, Jean, 32n56
Winchester, bishop of, 63
Wolsey, Thomas, cardinal, 26
women, right to succession, 30–31; psychology of, 31; not in pageants? 56n109
Wood Street, 49
Wriothesley, Charles, Windsor Herald, 16, 101
Wyatt's Rebellion, 43
Wygge, Robert, 118
York, 24, 25, 67; archbishop of, 105

Publications of the Centre for Reformation and Renaissance Studies

Renaissance and Reformation Texts in Translation

Du Bellay, Ronsard, Sébillet. *Poetry and Language in 16th-Century France*. Trans. and Intro. by Laura Willett (2004), pp. 116. ISBN 0-7727-2021-5

Girolamo Savonarola. *A Guide to Righteous Living and Other Works*. Trans. and Intro. by Konrad Eisenbichler (2003), pp. 243. ISBN 0-7727-2020-7

Godly Magistrates and Church Order: Johannes Brenz and the Establishment of the Lutheran Territorial Church in Germany, 1524-1559. Trans. & Ed. J.M. Estes (2001), pp. 219. ISBN 0-7727-2017-7

Giovanni Della Casa. *Galateo: A Renaissance Treatise on Manners*. Trans. & Ed. K. Eisenbichler and K.R. Bartlett. 3rd ed. (2001), pp. 98. ISBN 0-9697512-2-2

Romeo and Juliet Before Shakespeare: Four Stories of Star-Crossed Love. Trans. & Ed. N. Prunster (2000), pp. 127. ISBN 0-7727-2015-0

Jean Bodin. *On the Demon-Mania of Witches*. Abridged, trans. & ed. R.A. Scott and J.L. Pearl (1995), pp. 219. ISBN 0-9697512-5-7

Whether Secular Government Has the Right to Wield the Sword in Matters of Faith: A Controversy in Nürnberg in 1530. Five Documents trans. & Ed J.M. Estes (1994), pp. 118. ISBN 0-9697512-4-9

Lorenzo Valla. *'The Profession of the Religious' and Selections from 'The Falsely-Believed and Forged Donation of Constantine'*. Trans. & ed. O.Z. Pugliese. 2nd ed. (1994), pp. 114. ISBN 0-9697512-3-0

A. Karlstadt, H. Emser, J. Eck. *A Reformation Debate: Karlstadt, Emser and Eck on Sacred Images*. Trans. & Ed. B. Mangrum and G. Scavizzi. 2nd edition (1991), pp. 112. ISBN 0-9697512-7-3

Nicholas of Cusa. *The Layman on Wisdom and the Mind*. Trans. M.L. Führer (1989) pp. 112. ISBN 0-919473-56-3

Bernardino Ochino. *Seven Dialogues*. Trans. & Ed. R. Belladonna (1988), pp. xlviii, 96. ISBN 0-919473-63-6

Tudor and Stuart Texts

Early Stuart Pastoral: 'The Shepherd's Pipe' by William Browne and others, and *'The Shepherd's Hunting' by George Wither*. Ed. & Intro by J. Doelman (1999), pp. 196. ISBN 0-9697512-9-X

The Trial of Nicholas Throckmorton. A modernized edition. Ed. & Intro by A. Patterson. (1998), pp. 108. ISBN 0-9697512-8-1

James I. *The True Law of Free Monarchies* and *Basilikon Doron*. Ed. & Intro by D. Fischlin and M. Fortier (1996), pp. 181. ISBN 0-9697512-6-5

Essays and Studies

Shell Games: Studies in Scams, Frauds, and Deceits (1300-1650). Ed. Mark Crane, Richard Raiswell, and Margaret Reeves. (2004), pp. 320. ISBN 0-7727-2023-1

A Renaissance of Conflicts: Visions and Revisions of Law and Society in Italy and Spain. Ed. John Marino and Thomas Kuehn. (2004), pp. 456. ISBN 0-7727-2022-3.

The Renaissance in the Nineteenth Century / Le XIXe siècle renaissant. Ed. Y. Portebois and N. Terpstra (2003), pp. 302. ISBN 0-7727-2019-3

The Premodern Teenager: Youth in Society 1150-1650. Ed. K. Eisenbichler (2002), pp. 349. ISBN 0-7727-2018-5

Occasional Publications

Annotated Catalogue of Editions of Erasmus at the Centre for Reformation and Renaissance Studies, Toronto. Comp. J. Glomski and E. Rummel (1994), pp. 153. ISBN 0-9697512-1-4

Register of Sermons Preached at St. Paul's Cross (1534-1642). Comp. M. MacLure. Revised by P. Pauls and J.C. Boswell (1989), pp. 152. ISBN 0-919473-48-2

Language and Literature. Early Printed Books at the CRRS. Comp. W.R. Bowen and K. Eisenbichler (1986), pp. ix, 112. ISBN 0-7727-2009-6

Published Books (1499-1700) on Science, Medicine and Natural History at the CRRS Comp. W.R. Bowen and K. Eisenbichler (1986), pp. ix, 35. ISBN 0-7727-2005-3

Bibles, Theological Treatises and Other Religious Literature, 1492-1700, at the CRRS. Comp. K. Eisenbichler et al. (1981), pp. 94. ISBN 0-7727-2002-9

Humanist Editions of Statutes and Histories at the CRRS. Comp. K. Eisenbichler et al. (1980), pp. xxi, 63. ISBN 0-7727-2001-0

Humanist Editions of the Classics at the CRRS. Comp. N.L. Anderson et al. (1979), pp. ix, 71. ISBN

To order books, and for additional information, contact:
CRRS Publications, Victoria University
71 Queen's Park, Toronto ON, M5S 1K7, CANADA
tel: (416) 585-4465 / fax: (416) 585-4430
e-mail: crrs.publications@utoronto.ca / web: www.crrs.ca